Pacific Press® Publishing Association
Nampa, Idaho
Oshawa, Ontario, Canada
www.pacificpress.com

Copyright 2007 by Pacific Press® Publishing Association
Printed in the United States of America
All rights reserved

Cover design by Gerald Lee Monks
Cover Illustration by Lars Justinen
Inside design by Steve Lanto

Unless otherwise noted, Scripture quotations are from the Holy Bible, English Standard Version, copyright © 2001 by Crossway Bibles, a division of Good News Publishers.

Scripture quotations credited to the NIV are from the HOLY BIBLE, NEW INTERNATIONAL VERSION, copyright © 1973, 1978, 1984 International Bible Society. Used by permission of Zondervan Bible Publishers.

Scripture quotations credited to KJV are from the King James Version of the Bible.

Scripture quotations credited to *The Message* are copyright © 1993, 1994, 1995, 1996, 2000, 2001, 2002 by Eugene H. Peterson. Used by permission of NavPress Publishing Group.

Library of Congress Cataloging-in-Publication Data

Pierce, Seth J.
What we believe for teens / Seth J. Pierce.
p. cm.
ISBN 13: 978-0-8163-2213-8 (pbk.)
ISBN 10: 0-8163-2213-9 (pbk.)
1. Seventh-day Adventists--Doctrines--Juvenile literature. I. Title.
BX6154.P4 85 2007
230'.6732--dc22
                                                          2007013319

Additional copies of this book are available by calling toll-free 1-800-765-6955 or by visiting http://www.adventistbookcenter.com.

11 12 13 • 07 06 05

Dedication

To my dad, whose advice and insights always
challenge me to be Christ-centered; and to his
warped sense of humor, which has found its way into my writing.
I love you.

Acknowledgments

The fact that anything I write has even one coherent thought demands major props and appreciation to my Lord Jesus Christ. He continues to amaze me in how good He is. Secondly, I need to give some love to some of His people, who have helped me along the way. Thank you to my wonderful wife, Angela, whose love and affection is a constant source of encouragement. Thanks to John Reeve for his insights on the Trinity; and to Jeff Carlson for e-mailing me that war story during class at the risk of great peril to his academic future. Thanks to Summer Howell and her parents, Greg and Melissa, for their faithful friendship. Thanks to *all* my Union College friends (and those with the Union spirit!), who are suffering for their faith in Berrien Springs for various reasons. I would also like to thank Myrna Bowie, who does my taxes for me, for the meager sum of an autographed book. You're incredible. Of course I cannot forget the usual suspects who have helped me along the way, such as the Value Menu at Taco Bell, the Internet (eBay and Half.com), books, *Calvin and Hobbes*, Johnny Depp (thanks for taking the time to listen), Catherine Zeta-Jones (next time I'll pay for lunch!), Batman (for inspiring me to get involved in my community), and the soon-to-be-released *Transformers* movie because that looks awesome. I also have a deep appreciation for everyone at *The Office*, anyone who has been hit with a ball in the head and/or crotch on national television because that is still the funniest thing in the world, and shampoo. Also, I need to mention all the "pony questions" that derailed lectures long enough for me to write a few pages on this project during class. Thank you, one and all!

Table of Contents

1. The Holy Scriptures 9
2. The Trinity.. 16
3. The Father.. 21
4. The Son.. 27
5. The Holy Spirit 32
6. Creation 38
7. The Nature of Man 43
8. The Great Controversy.. 49
9. The Life, Death, and Resurrection of Christ................ 57
10. The Experience of Salvation 61
11. Growing in Christ... 67
12. The Church.. 72
13. The Remnant and Its Mission 78
14. Unity in the Body of Christ 86
15. Baptism.. 91
16. The Lord's Supper 97
17. Spiritual Gifts and Ministries 102
18. The Gift of Prophecy.. 108
19. The Law of God 116
20. The Sabbath 122
21. Stewardship... 128
22. Christian Behavior 134
23. Marriage and the Family 140
24. Christ's Ministry in the Heavenly Sanctuary 145
25. The Second Coming... 154
26. Death and Resurrection... 161
27. The Millennium and the End of Sin............................. 167
28. The New Earth 173

1 | The Holy Scriptures

I don't know what was different about that night; for some reason my brothers and I did not want to go to sleep. My brother Ben, my stepbrother T. J., and I had all been marched through the bathroom and then downstairs to our bedroom and told it was time to go to bed. I decided to mount a resistance.

We owned a collection of toys known as Sky Commanders—plastic spaceships and battle stations that fired plastic missiles. They had zip lines attached to the ceiling so you could send the ships whizzing across the room at your target while they fired the plastic missiles. I determined these toys would be the answer to our parents' power trip—I mean, who were they to tell us when to go to bed? How much power did they really have?

So I gave a rousing speech to my siblings. "We can defeat our parents if you will follow me and my plan! We will use our Sky Commanders to mount a resistance—it will be a devastating attack! Our parents will be weeping and apologizing for sending us to bed." My brothers believed me and took my speech as absolute truth. Together we set up our attack.

What We Believe

When everything was in place, we made a lot of noise so as to rouse our parents from their slumber. Soon we could hear the *thump, thump, thump* of footsteps coming down the stairs. Dad was coming, and he would be angry.

"Battle stations!" I hissed in a loud whisper. Everyone ran to a different corner of the room, readying their equipment.

"Lights!" I hissed again, and the room was in utter darkness. "Wait for it—"

When my dad opened the door expecting to have to give yet another lecture to us wayward children, he was greeted by a surprise. Total darkness. He fumbled around until he found the switch and the lights came on. He was taken aback by what he saw.

Zip lines were strung all over the rafters, with spaceships ready to fly; a whole army of futuristic plastic canons was arranged all over the floor. And manning all the toy weaponry were three very stupid children semifrozen with fear. My dad took a step back.

"What the—"

"FIRE!" I shouted, hoping that one of my siblings would have the guts to do something, since I was paralyzed at that moment by the absurdity of what we were doing. See, my dad is a black belt in martial arts, and it dawned on me that three kids and their toys probably weren't going to be the most effective negotiation tool to use. Thankfully, Ben came unfrozen enough to fire one red missile, which bounced off my dad's shoulder.

Bad idea. Really bad.

My dad was so angry at what we were doing that he single-handedly tore down all the spaceships and kicked over all our battlements in a few seconds, throwing them all into the toy box.

"Our toys!" we cried as we saw them crash into each other as they flew into the toy box. "Our beautiful toys!" Once my dad had finished dismantling our assault, he told us to get back to bed and mumbled something about "dumber than a box of rocks" as he returned to his bedroom.

I had to bear the icy glares of my siblings for a few days and lost a great deal of power as they realized that, even though I was the oldest, my advice and ideas were not always good and they should be taken with caution.

The Holy Scriptures

You'll find a lot of bad advice in this world—and even more bad ideas. And when followed, they can result in shame and pain. They may cause whatever situation we are trying to get out of to become even worse.

Recently I read a story of a pastor who claimed he could walk on water. Now we can admire this man's faith, but common sense tells us that while his faith may be admirable, his intelligence is not. In August of 2006, this thirty-five-year-old pastor insisted that anyone could literally walk on water, if only one had enough faith. Big and bold was his speech. He extolled the heavenly power possessed by a faithful man with such force that he may well have convinced himself. The pastor set out to walk across a major estuary. But he could not swim. Long story short, he sank like a rock straight to the bottom, only to emerge just in time for his funeral.

Bad thinking and advice are just everywhere. That same year in Wesley Chapel, Florida, a man was hit in the leg with pieces of the bullet he fired at the exhaust pipe of his car. While repairing the car, he needed to bore a hole in the pipe. When he couldn't find a drill, he tried to shoot a hole in it. I ask you, where do these people get their ideas?

For other examples of bad advice, we can consider the kid who has been having a hard time so his friends suggest getting drunk (which is a depressant). Not a good idea. Then there are the people who get dumped or hurt in a relationship, so they either avoid relationships altogether out of bitterness or get into one relationship right after another in order to fill the emptiness in their life. Another bad idea. Then there are those times in our life that cause us confusion, and because we are confused, we just don't do anything, which is seldom helpful. The list could go on and on.

Thankfully God has given us a tool that helps us when we need a good idea or we need some solid advice when we encounter the challenging, frustrating, and confusing times of life.

> "All Scripture is God-breathed and is useful for teaching, rebuking, correcting and training in righteousness, so that the man of God may be thoroughly equipped for every good work" (2 Timothy 3:16, 17, NIV).

What We Believe

He has given us Scripture—also known as God's Word and the Bible. It provides guidelines, advice, ideas, and comfort for any situation in life that we could encounter. Now, I realize that a book may not seem like the answer to your problems, but the Bible is not an ordinary book. It is unique—nothing compares to it. Just consider these facts.

This Book was written over a period of fifteen hundred years by more than forty authors from all walks of life—from kings to farmers. This doesn't mean that the Bible is human in origin—the Bible tells us it's not. But what it does mean is that God chose to express Himself using human words written by human hands. The Bible says "men spoke from God as they were carried along by the Holy Spirit" (2 Peter 1:21, NIV). God influenced the hearts and thoughts of human beings and helped them put into words what He wanted us to know. Incredible thought, huh?

The Holy Scriptures were written in different times, during war as well as peace, and crafted on three different continents—Asia, Africa, and Europe. They were written in three different languages—Hebrew, Aramaic, and Greek. There are more manuscripts (very old copies) to support the validity of the Scriptures than all other classical literature combined. The Bible is currently translated into more than two thousand languages. But the most amazing thing? Despite all its unique factors, *Scripture tells a single unfolding story.* Which brings me to the most impressive part of its uniqueness—the power of the story it tells.

> *Do you think God can still influence our hearts and minds today with the kind of wisdom we see in the Bible?*

First, you must know that the content of the Bible has caused the death of many people. It is important to notice that people have willingly died horrible deaths rather than denounce the Bible, while others have died horrible deaths just to get it into other people's hands. No simple story book could motivate that kind of commitment, which tells us that there is something special about what's inside its pages.

The Holy Scriptures

People have also killed because of the Bible. I'm not holding this up as a positive example to follow; but, to me, it just lends more weight to the idea that the Bible contains a message that moves people like no other book. And then there is the fact that no one can stop this Book; and many have tried. The Bible always triumphs.

A classic example of this was what happened to the French infidel Voltaire, who died in 1778. He told people that one hundred years from his time, Christianity would be swept from existence and pass into history. And what ended up happening? Fifty years after his death, the Geneva Bible Society used Voltaire's house to produce Bibles. Today, millions of Bibles are circulated, while Voltaire has simply passed into history. God's Word is powerful.

> "For the word of God is living and active, sharper than any two-edged sword, piercing to the division of soul and of spirit, of joints and of marrow, and discerning the thoughts and intentions of the heart" (Hebrews 4:12, NIV).

The ability of the Bible to remain a single unit despite its diverse origins, its ability to move people, and its ability to survive persecution are just a few factors that demonstrate this unique Book's power. And in the text above we see that it is living and active and can have an impact on us right down to our hearts and thoughts.

According to 2 Timothy 3:16, 17 we see that it has a use: to instruct us in our daily lives as we learn to live a life like Christ's. It's our instruction manual for life—and I'm glad God has given it to us.

Have you ever tried building something without the manual? When I was first married, my mom said that my wife and I could have her entertainment center. It was a nice big wooden structure and had lots of drawers and such—but no manual. It took a good while to take the thing apart, and when I moved it to my house it took . . . well . . . a very long time to piece everything back together.

God knows how hard it is to make sense of life with all its pieces, which is why He gave us a book, the Bible, that teaches, corrects, and equips us to build a righteous life. This Book has shaped countless

What We Believe

millions of lives. It has always come through for me when I needed wisdom. It is the only source of foolproof wisdom there is.

It is comforting to know that we have an instruction manual for life in the Bible. It gives us advice on everything you could ever need. God's Word will always come through for you and help you have victory, success, and hope in every area of your life if you put its contents into practice—and that is a lot more than I can say for Sky Commanders and older brothers.

READ IT FOR YOURSELF

Before you begin reading the Holy Scriptures, I must warn you that it won't work if you read it like an ordinary book. Because it is unique and special, we must approach the Bible in a different way than other books if we are to gain understanding from it and hear God speak to us. Here are a few suggestions to help you read your Bible.

First, always ask God to send you the Holy Spirit to help you understand what the Bible says. The Bible is full of deep spiritual knowledge, and in order to find it, you will need the help of the Spirit of God. "The man without the Spirit does not accept the things that come from the Spirit of God, for they are foolishness to him, and he cannot understand them, because they are spiritually discerned" (1 Corinthians 2:14, NIV).

Second, the goal of reading the Bible is not to memorize facts or to learn history. Go buy a history book on the Middle East if that's what you're interested in. The Bible is not a textbook, a history book, or any other kind of book full of information to be memorized. Unfortunately, a lot of people think they become more spiritual by how *much* of the Bible they read, while not understanding any of it. If you take what the Bible says as advice, one little phrase can change your life or have you studying for weeks to determine its meaning. When you study, do it to get new understanding from God. Read a few verses and then ask some questions about it. It might be a good idea to get a Bible commentary or Bible dictionary to help you gain even more understanding into the passage you're reading.

Third, meditate on (think about) what you've read. Roll it around in your brain for a while and then ask God, "What is it You are trying to tell me through this passage?" Then wait for God to impress your thoughts with holy ideas of how He wants you to apply what you have read to your life. " 'But the one who hears my words and does not put them into practice is like a man who built a house on the ground without a foundation. The moment the torrent struck that house, it collapsed and its destruction was complete' " (Luke 6:49, NIV).

God's Word can't help you unless you apply it to your life. You may not always like what you hear—it might make you uncomfortable or make you have to change the way you do things—but it will always work for your benefit.

2 | The Trinity

I stink at math. No, it's true. When I was in junior high and high school, I took to arithmetic like a fish to basketball. I stink at basketball too, but that's another story. It wasn't always this way. There was a time when I understood math concepts, but around the fourth grade I noticed my confidence waning. I came to this realization during an anxiety-ridden game known to cause asthma attacks, panic attacks, vertigo, seizures, and nervous twitching—at least in me—a game known as Around the World.

The object of this exercise in exasperation was for one student to start at one end of the classroom and go desk to desk in a head-to-head competition with other students. The teacher would hold up a math flashcard, and the roaming student (the one going desk to desk or "around the world") would try to shout out the answer before the student sitting in the desk would. If he or she succeeded, the roaming student would move to the next desk in hopes of defeating the next student. If the roaming student was faster than all the other students, they would win, having gone "around the world." But if a student in a desk barked out the correct sum before the roaming student, then the roaming student

The Trinity

would return to their desk of origin and the student who defeated them would begin their journey. Sound fun? Well, it was until you got to the last few desks.

When I had only a few desks to go, a mixture of pressure and excitement swirled around my stomach. A swell of anxiety found its way into my brain, and when I saw the flashcard I would either shout the right answer (startling everyone in every class in the small school I went to), or burble incoherent idiocies that nobody understood except me, and I would be defeated. I only won a few times, and then I had to excuse myself to the bathroom, or the nurses' office, to recuperate. So by the time I hit fifth grade I already had a healthy anxiety with math. To make matters worse, I was greeted by an even greater evil in my new textbook than the game around the world.

I was alarmed in fifth grade because my A-B-Cs started mixing with my 1-2-3s in an unnatural union known as algebra. It's downright perverse. I mean, how does $35 + w = 93$? What's that W doing out of the alphabet? And what about $x - y = 17$? How can y be subtracted from x when y is the twenty-fifth letter in the alphabet and x is only the twenty-fourth? And even then, shouldn't the answer be 1? Where did 17 come from? And so began my downward spiral in math. I was asked to solve one abysmal abomination after another, including fractions, radius, diameter, and equations in a variety of unsavory subjects such as geometry, calculus, and of course, algebra. And as I slowly finished my math classes in high school and college I was so delighted I would never have to consider the stuff ever again—save the very basics. But as I studied the Bible, the more I was confronted with a hard reality. The Bible—God's Word—has some very crazy math.

Just consider the following examples. Genesis 1:1, 2 says, "In the beginning, God created the heavens and the earth. The earth was without form and void, and darkness was over the face of the deep." The chapter goes on to explain how God created life as we know it. Now how did He do that? There was nothing there save maybe a floating rock and some water. In other words, God made something from nothing. That doesn't work in any math I know.

What We Believe

And what about Jesus? He was notorious for doing multiplication.

" 'We have no more than five loaves and two fish—unless we go and buy food for all these people.' For there were about five thousand men. . . . And taking the five loaves and two fish he [Jesus] looked up to heaven and said a blessing over them. . . . And they all ate and were satisfied" (Luke 9:13, 14, 16, 17). Jesus multiplied something the size of a Happy Meal into a banquet for thousands.

Then of course Jesus also cancels our debts of sin (look up 1 John 1:9). How many banks do you know that cancel people's debts because they love them? What kind of math is God doing? Then there is the classic statement Jesus makes in Revelation 22:13, where He calls Himself the "Alpha and Omega," which means the beginning and the end. Now I can understand how someone can have a beginning and have an end; but how can they *be* the beginning and the end? It's perplexing.

But perhaps there is no equation more perplexing than that of the Trinity. In the Bible we find an insight into the character and unity of God that is difficult to wrap our minds around. In Deuteronomy 6:4 we are given the statement, " 'Hear, O Israel: The Lord our God, the Lord is one.' " OK, it would appear we are working with the number 1—God is One. And as Christians we believe there is only one God—easy equation, right? Well, look at this next text.

Speaking of Jesus Christ, the Son of God, the Gospel writer says, "In the beginning was the Word, and the Word was with God, and the Word was God" (John 1:1). And just in case you're tempted to think the Word was someone other than Jesus, John goes on to say, "And the Word became flesh and dwelt among us, and we have seen his glory, glory as of the only Son from the Father, full of grace and truth. . . . For the law was given through Moses; grace and truth came through Jesus Christ" (verses 14, 17). The Bible says Jesus is God. Jesus Himself says it: " 'I and the Father are one' " (John 10:30). But as we saw in Deuteronomy, God (referred to as the Father in John 1 and elsewhere in the Bible) is One. So we are working with the equation (2 = 1). Confused yet? Great, let's continue.

When Jesus was baptized in the Jordan River by John the Baptist, we not only see the Son and God the Father, but we see a third party come

The Trinity

into play. "And when Jesus was baptized, immediately he went up from the water, and behold, the heavens were opened to him, and he saw [now pay attention here] the Spirit of God descending like a dove and coming to rest on him; and behold a voice *from heaven* said, This is my beloved Son, with whom I am well pleased" (Matthew 3:16, 17; emphasis added). Now, how do you like them apples? There are Three—count them—Three divine Beings interacting in this passage: Jesus the Son of God, the Spirit of God, and the Father God. And in Matthew 28:19 we see Jesus telling His disciples to actually baptize people in the name of the " 'Father and of the Son and of the Holy Spirit.' " All Three Names are equated with each Other. Paul, in his letter to the Corinthians, ends by saying, "The grace of the Lord Jesus Christ and the love of God and the fellowship of the Holy Spirit be with you all" (2 Corinthians 13:14).

Clearly, Three divine Entities work with each Other here, and yet the Bible insists that there is only ONE Lord, ONE Spirit, and ONE God (Ephesians 4:4–7) and that we are to give glory and honor to the ONLY God (1 Timothy 1:17). Call me a cotton-headed ninnymuggins, but it appears that we are dealing with an equation that says 3 = 1. How do we make sense of this? You tell me.

People have tried to crack this code for centuries. This math problem has gone "around the world," and while we have theories galore, no one has been able to come up with a definitive explanation about how this works. What we do have is the term *Trinity*, a term that simply refers to what we see in the Bible, a Three-in-One God. One God who has revealed Himself three different ways, and each of those ways has the same "Godness" as the others. The term *Trinity* does not explain how this works. Make you a little uncomfortable? Don't let it. Just look at it from another perspective.

> *How does God revealing Himself help you understand and relate to Him better?*

Consider Jesus' own words about Himself being the Alpha and Omega. Jesus has eternal life and offers us the same. Now you could pull out the old dictionary and look up the word *eternal* or *eternity* and come up with a definition that would say "indefinite" or "goes on and on without end" or "the seeming length of most math classes" (sorry). And while we understand what eternity refers to, does anyone really grasp what eternity feels like? Is it possible to really understand it? Having no beginning and no end? I think the oldest person I ever heard of lived to 120, which is nothing compared to eternity. Just because we use terms to refer to something doesn't mean we understand them completely.

Then consider this other perspective. Life is complex. It took us thousands of years just to create a sheep and then it was a clone—a copy. One sheep! But life is so complex, with its atoms, cells, microscopic processes, mood swings, and dietary preferences, that we have barely scratched the surface of what it means to be alive and create living things. Even blades of grass are complicated. So my question to you is, should we expect the Author of Life to be any less complex?

God chose to reveal Himself in three different ways so we could have a better picture of what He is like, with all His facets and character traits. The very thing that puzzles us gives us a clearer picture of God.

I still stink at math, and I don't know if I'll ever understand 3 = 1. But I know that when I get to heaven I'll have an eternity to learn and study all about God. And that is one subject I am willing to do a little math in.

3 | The Father

A few years ago I came across a news story about a dad who did something a little different in order to convince a judge that he should have custody of his children. Since it was a long time ago I don't remember the man's name, but we'll call him George. George lived in the United Kingdom and had been through a nasty divorce.

While George wasn't so much concerned about having his wife back, he wanted his children to come live with him. The court did not agree. Devastated, George knew he had to do something to prove that he was a good dad. He had to prove that he was worthy of the responsibility of raising his impressionable children.

So you can imagine what he did. That's right, he dressed up like Spiderman.

For reasons I could never hope to comprehend, George donned the suit of the famous superhero, and (that's right, there's more!) climbed up a *huge* crane hovering over a major intersection of the city. I mean, come on, where else would Spiderma—I mean Spiderdad go, right?

Spiderdad sat up there to protest the fact that the court had refused him the right to raise his children. Needless to say, when the authorities

What We Believe

dragged Spiderdad off the crane, they reaffirmed their commitment to keeping his children away from him; and perhaps any child for that matter. Next time maybe he should think things through a little bit . . . or dress up like Batman, because I'm sure that would work.

There are some "bad dads" out there. In another story of a dad gone bad, a Minnesota man had 114 explosives and 20 pounds of combustible powder, along with some tidy instructions for creating bombs, in his house. He—along with his family he was supposed be the leader of—were arrested and faced twenty thousand dollars in fines and ten years in prison each for their terroristlike hobby. Definitely a bad dad.

There are too many stories of fathers who harm the ones they are called to love and guide. There are fathers who verbally and sexually abuse their family members, ones who abandon them, ones who refuse to work and earn money to take care of them, and ones who are about as loving and kind as the needles on the back of an angry porcupine. But, while there are bad dads running loose in society (as well as sitting in jail cells), there are plenty of good dads as well.

Recently a movie based on a true story about a good dad was released starring Will Smith. It's called *The Pursuit of Happyness* and it chronicles the life of a man named Chris Gardner, a poor, struggling young man who ended up homeless and yet does everything in his power to provide for his young son. In the end, after a lot of heartache, tears, and toil, Chris finally succeeds as a businessman and is able to provide a good life for his beloved son. It is a stirring story about the love of a father for his son and the strength of human will to succeed. And the best part is that it actually happened. Chris Gardner is alive and well today as a multimillionaire who donates heavily to the church and soup kitchen that helped him when he was homeless. And there are other great dads too. They may not have a movie made about their life, but they do things every day to make the lives of their loved ones special.

Many people can tell you how their dad taught them about life, helped them with their homework, helped them learn how to drive, played games with them, taught them how to throw a ball, and even taught them about God. And yet, even good dads struggle sometimes.

In his best-selling book *The Five People You Meet in Heaven*, Mitch Albom gives a profound analogy for fatherhood. The book is a fictional account of a man named Eddie and what happens when he dies in a tragic carnival accident and goes to heaven. While the book definitely deviates from the Bible in terms of the afterlife (see chapter 26 on what happens when a person dies), it does manage to paint some poignant pictures. In the book, when you get to heaven, you do not meet God right away; instead you encounter five people. These five people are folks who at some point in your life affected you and you them. Their job is to tell you what your life meant and how it affected them. They paint a picture for Eddie to help him understand his reason for living. One of those people talks to Eddie about his father.

In the book we get a glimpse into Eddie's past and see how abusive his father was to him. And it is here that Mitch Albom uses a powerful insight into fatherhood. He states that, not just bad dads, but "all fathers hurt their children." Then he gives us an analogy. He says that each child is like a pristine glass vase in their father's hands. Some fathers leave fingerprints and others leave smudges. But there are some who squeeze the vase so hard, or treat it so recklessly, it shatters into a thousand jagged little pieces.

I'm sorry to say that Mitch's analogy is true—no matter how good a father is, he isn't perfect. They impart their good qualities but also some negative ones. And some have turned their kids into jagged little shards that cut and hurt just as they have been cut and hurt. I've met some—and it is heartbreaking. The Bible says that "all have sinned and fall short of the glory of God" (Romans 3:23, NIV)—even moms and dads. And because of this sad reality, it makes me wonder why God refers to Himself in the Bible as the Father.

When Jesus taught His disciples to pray, He started with, "Our Father which art in heaven" (Luke 11:2, KJV). And when Paul is writing to the church in Ephesus he says, "Blessed be the God and Father of our Lord Jesus Christ, who has blessed us in Christ with every spiritual

What We Believe

blessing in the heavenly places" (Ephesians 1:3). And these two texts are just a smidgeon of all the ones used by both Jesus (the Son of the Father God) and the followers of Jesus. What gives? Didn't they have bad fathers back then? You bet your bippy they did.

Two notable bad dads in the Bible had to be Noah and Lot. Noah, after being used mightily by God to save humanity from the Flood using a giant boat, went and got drunk. What a great example. "That's right, kids, do what the Lord wants, and then go drink yourself into a stupor." To make matters worse, he got so drunk that he lost all of his clothes (look up Genesis 9:21). Not exactly a message we want to teach kids, is it? And Lot was worse.

First of all, Lot moved his family to a city that was so bad God had to come down out of heaven to see it for Himself—and then He torched it with holy fire (look up Genesis 19:24). Good move, father Lot. But even before the holy burning, Lot demonstrated parenting skills that would rival Spiderdad.

When God first visited, He and a couple of angels stayed with Lot in his home. And when the evil men of the city came out to knock down Lot's doors so they could have their way with Lot's guests, Lot offered his two virgin daughters to the evil men determined to rape and hurt people (find it in Genesis 19:4–8). Thanks, Dad—way to sacrifice for your kids. And there are many other stories of guys in the Bible who wouldn't make honorable mention for Father of the Year. Yet God chooses to identify Himself as a father. Why?

> *How do you think our earthly fathers affect our perception of our heavenly Father?*

One reason is to help us relate better to God. God is the Creator, the Master of the universe, the Force from which all life and reality flow. He has no beginning and no end, and is so glorious in power that He told Moses, " 'you cannot see my face, for no one may see me and live' " (Exodus 33:20, NIV). How do we relate to someone so utterly otherworldly and holy? We're just little ants compared to God. So, God gave us a term that we are familiar with. And in the Bible the term *father* doesn't just mean parent, as if God were saying, "Yeah, I'm responsible

The Father

for your existence like a parent—but that's it." No, it means something more personal than that.

The word the Bible uses for Father is *Abba*. "For you did not receive a spirit that makes you a slave again to fear, but you received the Spirit of sonship. And by him we cry, '*Abba*, Father' " (Romans 8:15, NIV). The term *Abba* is an Aramaic word transliterated into Greek by the apostle Paul. It was a term used within the family circle, and was derived from the lips of infants (Can't you just hear the little babies cooing "Ab-bah!" in their little nonsense babble?). It suggests a great deal of trust and intimacy in a relationship. Some think it is the ancient equivalent of the term *daddy*. But what's in a name? Sure, God wants us to refer to Him that way—but is He really that good?

It's true that earthly dads make boo-boos here and there; but God is the original father. He is the ideal; He is perfect. And by calling Himself "Father" He wants not only to set an example for all earthly dads but to show us how great a father really is. And He does it well.

After all, it was the Father who sent His Son Jesus to save us from sin (John 3:16). It was the Father who created the world and the life it contains (Genesis 1:1). It was the Father who acts fairly and encourages others to act the same by giving us laws in biblical books like Exodus, Deuteronomy, and Leviticus. It is the Father who will give us victory over evil and death at the end of time (Revelation 19:1). And it is the Father who takes care of those who are fatherless, widowed, and feeling like they don't belong (Deuteronomy 8:10). He even takes note of every tear we cry (Psalm 56:8).

And for those whose earthly fathers have hurt them and broken them into jagged little pieces, the Bible calls God the Potter.

> Yet, O LORD, you are our Father.
> > We are the clay, you are the potter;
> > we are all the work of your hand (Isaiah 64:8, NIV).

God is the only Father who can wipe away the hurtful fingerprints and smudges left on our lives. He can even pick up the pieces of shattered lives and make them even better than new.

What We Believe

What a great Father!

The Bible says, " 'The Lord, the Lord, a God merciful and gracious, slow to anger, and abounding in steadfast love and faithfulness, keeping steadfast love for thousands, forgiving iniquity and transgression and sin, but who will by no means clear the guilty, visiting the iniquity of the fathers on the children and the children's children, to the third and the fourth generation' " (Exodus 34:6, 7). God is not only loving, He is also fair and just. He is balanced and perfect.

It amazes me that this Father, the Sum of All Reality, allows us to call Him Dad. It gives me hope to think that no matter who hurts me, or how much of a mess I make of my life, there is a heavenly Father who forgives me and helps me pick up the pieces. We are all children of God—a God who wants custody of us for eternity. And because He is the perfect Dad—as well as the perfect Judge—all we have to do is accept Him, and He will make a place for us in heaven to live with Him—forever. And that's even cooler than having Spiderman as your dad.

4 | The Son

Recently I went with some friends to an art museum in Chicago. More often than not I was confronted with pictures that left me clueless. One such picture was an oil painting of a large severed cow head hanging by a hook. As if that wasn't gorgeous enough, to complement the dangling bloody head was the corresponding tongue hanging next to it.

Gross.

I mean, what was the artist doing? What kind of person gets into art to paint severed cow heads? The goofy thing was this same painter had other lovely paintings of landscapes and people. Why didn't he paint another one of those?

Then came what I refer to as the "nonsense" paintings. Miscellaneous colors and shapes strewn together making absolutely no picture whatsoever. My more artistic friends—who are far more cultured than I—tell me things like "It's about the emotion behind the colors" or "It's abstract art" or "It's about the technique used to get those shapes, brushstrokes, and textures." It's about nonsense, is what it is. If you had that talent, why not paint things people understand? At least for simple artistically challenged people like me.

What We Believe

Then there are photographs. A great many of them have nice pictures of various things, but others are more special than especially good. I've even taken a few of these. There's nothing better than looking at a picture of my wife, her mom, her dad, and my massive thumb taking up half the picture. There are a lot of bad pictures out there—a lot of distorted ones from paintings to photos. But the worst distorted pictures are the ones that involve God.

The world is full of distorted pictures of God. Consider the fact that while some people praise the Lord's name, others use it as a curse word. Who is God? Someone to praise or someone to curse by? Then we have to consider the people who claim to follow God. They are His representatives, right? And yet in history we can see atrocities like the Crusades, where Christians went after Muslims in order to wipe them off the face of the earth. The church in the Middle Ages hunted down people who disagreed with them, strapped them to wooden posts, and burned them alive in view of church members. Can you imagine what people must have thought of God based on this?

And then there are Christians today. I am only a young pastor, but I have already seen some of the meanest, most judgmental, name-calling, unloving people you could ever hope to avoid . . . and they claimed to be Christians.

A few years ago an elderly man claiming to be a Christian began sending me hate mail. He called my ministry a "joke" and said I was nothing more than a "clown" and all sorts of mean things. Then he would sign his letters "Love, your brother in Christ." It was confusing. If this had been where I got my picture of God from, I would have thought God was critical and hurtful and only said "I love you" because it sounded nice—not because He meant it.

Another time, I was out witnessing on a street known for its bars frequented by college kids. Outside one of the bars a group of Christians were standing by a line of college kids screaming at them and calling them names like "whores," "whoremongers," and worse. Now how do you suppose those half-drunk college kids felt about God after seeing His followers scream names and judgment at them? Ironically enough, I found out later that the "Christians" were from a church called Glad Tidings.

The Son

Now certainly there are millions upon millions of wonderful Christians as well, but given the two varieties, just who is representing God? So many people are confused about God, angry at God, and afraid of God as a result of distorted pictures of Him, and as a result they paint distorted pictures of their own.

I don't know how many times I have seen God portrayed on television or in movies. Some portray Him as a white-haired old man who manipulates the world to His will, regardless of what humans want. He's controlling. Other pictures show disaster after disaster befalling the earth—and even though people cry out to God, He never shows up. He's distant. Still others show Him as compassionate and caring about people in the world. He's loving. How can we know what God is really like with all these different pictures? It's not a new problem.

In the Bible, confusion about God ran rampant as well. The religious leaders—the ones who were supposed to represent God—made all kinds of distorted pictures. According to the Bible they blamed people's handicaps and sicknesses on some secret sin of theirs or their parents (check John 9:2), exalted themselves over others (see Luke 18:11), and looked down on people who spent their time with those who needed help (look up Luke 15:2). They even cheated people in God's temple (see Matthew 21:12).

Based on the religious leaders' picture of God, folks in the Bible thought God was an exclusive, cruel, pompous, dishonest Deity who delighted in making life miserable. Makes that painting of a severed head and tongue look like a masterpiece compared to this distorted picture of God, doesn't it? Thankfully, God wasn't willing to have His awesome name tarnished and His character misrepresented, so He did some painting of His own and sent His Son Jesus to give us the real picture of what God is like.

"For God so loved the world, that he gave his only Son, that whoever believes in him should not perish but have eternal life" (John 3:16). God wanted us to know how much He loves us and how much He wants to be involved in our lives; so He poured Himself into His Son Jesus, who became human so He could walk, talk, and touch us and yet was completely God at the same time. "For in him all the fullness of

What We Believe

God was pleased to dwell" (Colossians 1:19). All God and all human at the same time? That's what the Bible says.

John's Gospel, in the very first chapter, says that *everything* was created through Jesus (John 1:3). He was active wa-a-a-ay back in Creation with God the Father. He flat-out claimed to be One with God (in John 10:30). Jesus also said, " 'I am the way and the truth and the life. No one comes to the Father except through me. If you really knew me, you would know my Father as well. From now on, you do know him and have seen him' " (John 14:6, 7, NIV). And yet we are told He put on humanity.

> *The Bible calls Jesus the "Son" of God. Why do you think He was given this title when Jesus is God Himself?*

He was born as a baby and was weak enough to be beaten and to bleed. He was human at the same time He was God. Make sense? I hope not, because I still don't get how He did it. I mean, *all* of God being put into one little baby? One little human? It's like pouring the ocean into a shot glass without spilling. I don't understand—but I'm glad it worked, because Jesus gave the world a beautiful picture of God.

While He was here Jesus touched the untouchable lepers; He stood up to religious bullies cheating people in the temple by throwing them out; He went out of His way to reach people the church wanted nothing to do with; He wept and marveled at the human experience, showing us that God is affected personally by our pain; He forgave the people who hurt Him; and then He made the greatest brushstroke of all in His portrait of God when He died for our sins, securing a place in eternity for all who want it.

" 'Whoever has seen me has seen the Father' " (John 14:9). Jesus is the perfect picture of God. And it is beautiful.

One of my favorite movies when I was little was *Mary Poppins*. You've probably seen the story of a nanny who had all sorts of magical powers and could take the children under her care, Jane and Michael, on wonderful adventures. One such adventure occurs on the streets of London when the children come across their friend, Burt, drawing lovely landscapes on the sidewalk with different-colored chalks.

The Son

After examining the pictures, Jane decides that they should all go into the picture portraying a lovely English countryside with a delightful carousel with shiny multicolored horses. Burt and Michael agree and they all look pleadingly at Mary Poppins. After a mild protest, she rolls her eyes and agrees. She tells them to hold hands and—after counting to that all-important number three—she jumps with them right into the chalk drawing. *Poof!* The next thing they know, they are gallivanting around the countryside, meeting new friends and entering a horse race, which Mary Poppins wins—of course.

Ever since I witnessed that scene I have tried, when I think no one's looking, to jump into drawings. The only scene I have managed to land in is an embarrassing one when my wife walks into the room and sees me standing atop a piece of artwork. But wouldn't it be cool to be able to jump into the most beautiful pictures and paintings you see?

Jesus thinks it would be cool to do that, so not only did He paint a beautiful picture of God but He painted one of heaven and of what it will be like to live there—and then He promised to come back again to pick us up and take us there to live in that beautiful scene forever.

> " 'In my Father's house are many rooms; if it were not so, I would have told you. I am going there to prepare a place for you. And if I go and prepare a place for you, I will come back and take you to be with me that you also may be where I am' " (John 14:2, 3, NIV).

We live in a world that can be stressful and difficult. It may cause us to wonder what God is doing or if He really cares. It's tempting to look at all the tragedy in the news and get a picture of life that seems as hopeless as trying to climb a waterfall and as gruesome as a painting of a severed cow head and tongue (I really didn't like that painting). Thankfully, the Bible records the life of Jesus. It tells us who He was and all the wonderful interactions He had with people. And whenever we feel discouragement and doubt regarding God's feelings toward us and the world, all we need to do is open the Bible and look at Jesus—because Jesus is the perfect picture of God.

5 | The Holy Spirit

When I was little I wanted to be Superman. I had a pair of bright blue pajamas with the Man of Steel's blazing red and yellow "S" logo on the chest and a fiery red cape that attached to the shoulders with Velcro. I would watch *Superman: the Movie* and then run around the house as fast as my skinny legs could carry me, to make the cape flap in the wind. I would hold my hands out in front of me like Superman did when he flew, and do laps around our house, which was round and had a circular hallway around a central staircase. I would hum the Superman theme song and make the all-important "swoosh" noises that absolutely must accompany a young boy pretending to break the sound barrier with his cotton/polyester-blend supersuit.

The highlight to this exercise in reckless imagination was when I made my final lap around the house and locked onto the couch as my final destination. Since I wasn't able to leap tall buildings in a single bound, I had to settle for leaping onto a couch. With a great jump I would spread myself out horizontal in mid-air, and for a moment, flight was mine! Then I would crash down into the pillows and be reminded of my lack of superpowers—that is, until I decided to become a Jedi knight.

The Holy Spirit

For a brief period in my life I would only answer to the name Luke Skywalker. I wanted so badly to wield a light saber and move things and control people with just a flick of the wrist. I wanted to be able to make superhuman leaps and survive deadly falls and choke the bad guys with just a gesture of my hand. Turns out the only light saber I ever managed to wield was made of plastic, which breaks when you smack stuff with it. All my hand gestures got me was a sore wrist, and whenever I tried to choke someone I got a time-out. I just didn't have the power.

I made a few more attempts ranging from He-Man ("Master of the Universe") to Teenage Mutant Ninja Turtles (couldn't grow a shell), but they all ended the same way. I didn't have any superpowers or mutations at my disposal for fighting evil.

Wouldn't it be great to have superpowers? Whose would you pick? But, guess what—there is no superpower in any comic book or movie that is accessible to us. However, the Bible tells us that we can have something far greater than a superpower—we can have supernatural power. We can have the same supernatural power that the greatest Hero of all time—Jesus Christ—had. Just consider a few of the things He did!

Jesus healed incurable diseases (Luke 8:43, 44); He overcame death (John 11:11–45); He defeated demons (Matthew 9:32, 33); He loved those who hated Him (Luke 23:34); He altered the known laws of nature (John 6:19; Mark 4:39). How, you ask? Because from His birth to His resurrection, Jesus possessed the Holy Spirit.

" 'Do not fear to take Mary as your wife, for that which is conceived in her is from the Holy Spirit. She will bear a son, and you shall call his name Jesus, for he will save his people from their sins' " (Matthew 1:20, 21). From the very beginning Jesus had this powerful Spirit from God in His life, and it was evident from the very beginning that He was powerfully different. As a preteen Jesus was brought to the temple, where all the wise old teachers hung out. He began conversing with them, and as a result of what Jesus as a boy said, the Bible tells us that "Everyone who heard him was amazed at his understanding and his answers" (Luke 2:47, NIV).

And when Jesus became an adult and was baptized in the Jordan River by John the Baptist we see, "And when Jesus was baptized, immediately he went up from the water, and behold, the heavens were opened to him, and he saw the Spirit of God descending like a dove and coming to rest on him" (Matthew 3:16). What was the result? Jesus began His ministry, and the miracles followed.

Lepers, the demon-possessed, and the dead were set free by Jesus through the power of the Spirit. People who were burnt out on God and who had been cheated by religious leaders found their faith renewed through Jesus' powerful Spirit-filled teaching. People who would have lived insignificant lives were transformed from fishermen and tax collectors into world-changing leaders and soul savers by the Holy Spirit's power working in the life of Jesus. It was what the Spirit came to do—heal, empower, and set free people whose lives were a trap of pain and aimlessness. Jesus declared, " 'The Spirit of the Lord is upon me, because he has anointed me to proclaim good news to the poor. He has sent me to proclaim liberty to the captives and recovering of sight to the blind, to set at liberty those who are oppressed' " (Luke 4:18).

And the best part is that what Jesus did, we can do too. Throughout Jesus' ministry He promises that " 'anyone who has faith in me will do what I have been doing. He will do even greater things than these, because I am going to the Father' " (John 14:12, NIV). It almost makes me excited enough to put on my old pajamas and try flying again!

And Jesus continues, explaining what will happen after He rises from the dead and returns to heaven. " 'And I will ask the Father, and he will give you another Helper, to be with you forever, even the Spirit of truth, whom the world cannot receive, because it neither sees him nor knows him. You know him, for he dwells with you and will be in you. I will not leave you as orphans; I will come to you' " (John 14:16–18). Jesus promises to send us the Holy Spirit to dwell in us so we can do even greater things than Christ did on earth!

I couldn't make up this stuff if I wanted to! It's right there, in the Bible, in black and white (or red and white, depending on your Bible).

So how do we get the Holy Spirit? And, really, what will we be able to do? The book of Acts is the place to be for questions like these.

As Jesus was ascending to heaven He gave some final instructions to His rag-tag bunch of followers. " 'But you will receive power when the

The Holy Spirit

Holy Spirit has come upon you, and you will be my witnesses in Jerusalem and in all Judea and Samaria, and to the end of the earth' " (Acts 1:8). OK, so they knew power from God was on the way and they would be empowered to share God's love to the end of the earth—but what to do in the meantime? Grab lunch? Take a walk? How does a person actually get ready to receive a gift like the Holy Spirit?

"And when the day of Pentecost was fully come, they were all with one accord in one place" (Acts 2:1, KJV). The idea here is that they were all gathered with a unity of hearts and minds patiently waiting—perhaps in prayer—for the Holy Spirit. Eventually He came. He came in cloven tongues of fire that rested on each follower of God and filled them with such power that they were enabled to preach in every language in the city. And as a result, three thousand people—in only one day—came to know Jesus Christ as their Savior. Wow! How many churches do you know can claim that kind of success? I don't even think I've talked to three thousand people this year, much less shared Christ with them.

> *How do you think we can receive the Holy Spirit?*

From then on the followers of God went to and fro performing miracles of healing (Acts 3:1–7) and sharing Jesus (Acts 14:21), as well as praying for people to receive the Holy Spirit (Acts 8:14–17) so they too could have the power of God in their life. And it doesn't matter who you are or what your shortcomings are—the Holy Spirit is available to you.

It's easy to look at ourselves and think about how little power we have. As human beings we are pretty pitiful. We fall down stairs and even up stairs; we tell lies; we get zits; we get angry; we lose things, forget things, and misplace things; we can get hurt, we feel fear, we feel stress; and we can feel out of control. We are extremely limited as well. We can't fly, and sometimes we can barely walk; we can't breathe underwater, and some of us can't even swim. Many of us need glasses, braces, and a colorful variety of medications. Could the Holy Spirit really empower us to be like Jesus?

Yes—yes, He can.

What We Believe

First off, the Holy Spirit has been working with humanity from the dawn of time, active with the Father and the Son even at Creation. See for yourself: "The earth was without form and void, and darkness was over the face of the deep. And the Spirit of God was hovering over the face of the waters" (Genesis 1:2). Thousands upon thousands of years ago before earth had grass, animals, or waterslides, God's Spirit was moving over the surface of our still shapeless home planet. This means that He has had thousands upon thousands of years' experience working with the hominids of God's handiwork—us. And just what has the Spirit been able to do with us since the dawn of life on earth? One thing's for sure: The Spirit has been anything but some abstract floating mystical substance. On the contrary, the Spirit interacted personally with us and has a history and a résumé that makes Him the best human development director of all time.

The Bible says the Spirit speaks to churches (Revelation 3:13), testifies of truth (1 John 5:6), brings Christ into our hearts (1 John 3:24), carries people's thoughts (2 Peter 1:21), rests on people (1 Peter 4:14), gives gifts (Hebrews 2:4), renews people's lives (Titus 3:5), dwells in us (2 Timothy 1:14), gives us power (Acts 1:8), gives joy, peace, and righteousness (Romans 14:17), reveals knowledge and transforms us into new people (1 Samuel 10:6) . . . and the list of the Holy Spirit's activities could go on and on.

However, the most important job the Spirit does is point us back to Jesus. " 'But when the Helper comes, whom I will send to you from the Father, the Spirit of truth, who proceeds from the Father, he will bear witness about me' " (John 15:26). Why would the Spirit bear witness to Jesus and not do some cool stuff on His own? Simple—because we are called to be like Jesus and follow Him. And there is a principle in the Bible that says the more we look and witness something—or someone, for that matter—the more we will become like them.

I must confess to you that I enjoy a good video game. I know there are better things to do, but I like being able to sit down with a plastic controller and take on the life of a jet pilot, a knight in shining armor, or any number of strange-looking cartoon characters that have come out of Japan in recent years. It's fun, but at the end of the day I am able to put down the controller (sometimes with a little effort) and get back

The Holy Spirit

to doing homework or writing books. But there are some people who can't. They don't have the power.

I was on the Internet a few years ago doing research (on a new video game) when I stumbled across a strange subculture called Cosplay. It's a combination of the words *costume* and *play*. Sounds like something for the little kiddies, doesn't it? But it isn't. As I looked at a few sites, I saw teens and middle-aged adults dressed in the bright colorful costumes—including the blue, pink, and eye-searing yellow hair—that adorns famous video game characters. It's a whole culture so enmeshed with video games and animation that they take on the identity of the game character—sometimes in clothes so bizarre that you have to avert your eyes.

Now I enjoy a good pair of Superman pajamas at bedtime, but to actually assume the identity of a video game character? On a regular basis? In public? These people have watched and played these games so much that they are trying to becoming like them.

Now, while I'm sure the parent that may be looking over you shoulder or perhaps reading you this chapter is tickled pink that I have painted video games in such a marvelous light, I hate to break it to you, but the issue isn't video games. People can become obsessed with television, health, looks, travel, work, and even working for God. The issue is our focus. What do we spend time looking at? Contemplating? Without the Holy Spirit in our hearts, it certainly isn't God.

The greatest work the Holy Spirit does in our hearts and minds is point us to Jesus. He reveals truths in the Bible. He impresses our hearts and minds with right thoughts and actions and transforms us to be like Christ so we can share His love more effectively.

> *What do you spend the most time thinking about? If you were asked what the focus and goal of your life is, what would you say?*

The Spirit worked with everyone from craftsmen (Exodus 35:30, 31) to the Christ (Luke 4:18); from strong men (Judges 15:14–20) to young men and women (Joel 2:28). You are perfectly suited to receive the Holy Spirit. The supernatural power of Jesus is available to you and everyone you know. I hope you will let Him in.

6 | Creation

Back in high school I had a science class with a non-Christian instructor. She was nice enough and much smarter than I. She seemed like a logical woman who didn't believe in fairy tales or God. But when it came to how human beings came into existence, she had some ideas that would have been right at home in a science-fiction novel.

"Humans," she told us, "came not just from monkeys but also from fish."

"Huh?"

"That's right, you see—millions of years ago the world was mostly water with fish living in it. The moon's gravitational pull pulled the waters into little pools here and there, leaving the fish trapped inside them. After a few more million years the fish grew legs and began walking around to look for food."

"Walking fish?"

"Yes. Then after some more millions of years they began to grow hair and became like monkeys."

"Monkey fish," I mumbled, not believing what I was hearing. "Then what happened?"

Creation

"Then the monkeys began to walk upright, lose their hair, and became humans!"

Wow.

If that wasn't the biggest bunch of hooey I had ever heard of. I respect science, and I believe it has given us invaluable insights into life on planet Earth, but at some point it seems to cease being science and turns into belief and faith. I mean, if my teacher was right, where are the records of the fish-monkey people? We should have some fossil or record of fish-monkey people somewhere, right? For me, I think the Bible offers a more plausible solution than nature somehow forming itself.

"In the beginning, God created the heavens and the earth" (Genesis 1:1). According to the Bible, nature didn't create itself or evolve—God made it. Now there are some who would say that God started the process of evolution but the plants, animals, and people still evolved. But the Bible again contradicts that theory by saying things like,

> And God said, "Let there be light," and there was light (Genesis 1:3).

> And God said, "Let there be an expanse in the midst of the waters, and let it separate the waters from the waters" (Genesis 1:6).

> So God created man in his own image, in the image of God he created him; male and female he created them (Genesis 1:27).

And there are a bunch more texts like these in Genesis 1. Amazing stuff is happening there. First of all, it says "God said" and then stuff happened—instantaneously. God is so powerful He can just speak things into existence. This really impresses me, especially when I consider Wahpeton, my cat.

Wahpeton is a good cat and a sweet cat, but sometimes I don't think he is a smart cat. I don't know how many times I have tried to get him to listen to me, to no avail.

What We Believe

I'll yell, "Wahpeton, get off the china cabinet!" And he just stares vacantly at me until I charge him, making lots of noise.

Other times I'll say, "Wahpeton, *no!*" when he is getting into something he shouldn't or stealing his brother Jag's food. He doesn't do anything until I physically remove him. He doesn't listen to a word I say! I've told him to get down, jump up, go away, come here, and pack me a lunch for school tomorrow, and he doesn't do any of it!

But God somehow can command the stars, the land, the waters, the animals, and all of nature—and they all obey Him. It's incredible. And according to the Bible, it took Him only six twenty-four-hour days to create them!

"And on the seventh day God finished his work that he had done, and he rested on the seventh day from all his work that he had done" (Genesis 2:2). Incredible. Now, do I understand how He did it?

Nope.

I don't understand the type of power it would take to speak a universe into existence when I can't even tell my cat to put a sock in it when he gets on one of his meowing binges—that's when he meows for no reason for fifteen minutes, which is worse than Chinese water torture.

Can you think of how God created the world? What kind of power did He use?

It reminds me of a passage in Psalms: "By the word of the LORD the heavens were made, and by the breath of his mouth all their host. He gathers the waters of the sea as a heap; he puts the deeps in storehouses. Let all the earth fear the LORD; let all the inhabitants of the world stand in awe of him!" (Psalm 33:6–8). God's creative powers are truly a wonder to behold! But this doesn't mean that we mindlessly stare in awe when people raise objections to Creation—no way. Christian scientists—and non-Christian scientists—have found plenty of evidence to suggest that the world didn't just happen by chance.

The Bible says, "The heavens declare the glory of God, / and the sky above proclaims his handiwork" (Psalm 19:1). In other words, things in nature and life give us clues to the fact that a divine hand was involved in creating the world. Look at just a couple of examples:

1. The fact that human beings, who are made in the image of God, enjoy beauty and creating things is a huge testimony to the fact that we have divine DNA. Fish-monkey people would have no use for paintings, music, or makeup, yet people are drawn to beauty—we love it. In evolution beauty is irrelevant, but to God who called His creation "very good," it matters. Since we have the fingerprints of God in our earth's history, it only makes sense that we like things that are "very good" as well.

2. In the book of Genesis, shortly after Creation comes the story of Noah, the man who built an ark and survived a worldwide cataclysmic flood. Today scientists have found evidence to suggest that it actually happened. They have found sea fossils way up in the mountains nowhere near the ocean—suggesting that waters once covered the whole earth. They have also found rock formations that look as though they were literally thrown together by a tremendous force. The Flood account says that waters deep in the earth were let loose to break through the ground. If that happened, then naturally you would see tremendously huge rocks thrown together in unnatural ways as tons of water was being jetted from the ground. Then there is the fact that while they differ a little at times, most major cultures in history have some form of a worldwide-flood story. So what does this have to do with Creation? Well, if the Bible was right on flood history, it would only makes sense that it wasn't lying when it recorded Creation history.

3. Probability is another indication that Someone special was at Creation. Could all life really come from nothing? Just evolve on its own? You've heard of one in a million, right? The probability of life as you see it now being the result of some random explosion in the past was tabulated by one mathematician to be

What We Believe

less than 1 in a number that begins with a 1 and has 3 million zeros after it. I don't know what you would even call a number like that, but it would probably take you a million years to count to it.

> *Do you think we will ever have enough evidence to absolutely prove God created the world?*

There are many more arguments like these for Creation versus some other theory. But the truth is there are lots of arguments against God being the Creator as well. What it boils down to is a willingness to study God's handiwork in nature and trust Him to provide you with answers you need as you learn more about Him. All arguments, from God to fish-monkey people, boil down to faith in the end. For all people the question is, "What do you want to put your faith in?"

7 | The Nature of Man

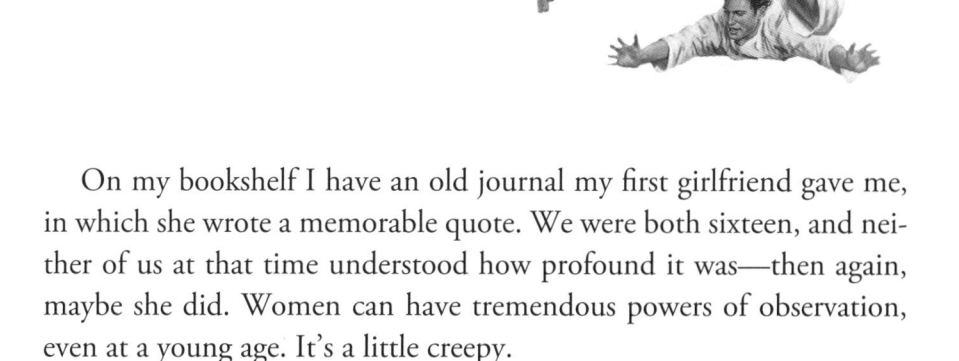

On my bookshelf I have an old journal my first girlfriend gave me, in which she wrote a memorable quote. We were both sixteen, and neither of us at that time understood how profound it was—then again, maybe she did. Women can have tremendous powers of observation, even at a young age. It's a little creepy.

The quote says, "You were born an original; don't die a copy." It was profound for me because I was living the exact opposite of the quote.

I wanted to be a rock star from the summer of 1994 to the winter of 1997. I wanted to play the guitar loud and proud in front of a bazillion screaming fans—all girls—and have a bazillion dollars. I had pictures of my favorite guitarists taped to the walls of my room, and I was determined to become what I saw in those images. I wanted to conform my life to the ones I saw performing on stage.

I started wearing the same clothes as the images in those posters did; I learned electric guitar; and I even grew my hair out down to the middle of my back (I'm not kidding). I did everything in my power to become that rock star. I just had to be that image! My life, as far as I was concerned, was going to be a carbon copy of the guitarist for Metallica.

43

What We Believe

Images are powerful. We see something and we want to be it. That's why companies advertise products using beautiful people. We see shampoo or a can of soda held up by a supermodel and think, *Wow, I want to look like that! If I only had that soda/shampoo/piece of clothing/fill in the blank.* The problem is that most of the images we try to become like by buying certain things or copying certain superstars will always leave us unfulfilled. The reason is simple—we have only *one* image we were designed to imitate, and that image belongs to God.

The Bible says that when God decided to create people He said, " 'Let us make man in our image, after our likeness' " (Genesis 1:26). God designed us to be like Him and to follow the things that are pleasing to Him. We are unique because we were made in God's image.

One character trait that distinguishes God (and us) over all creation is our individuality. The Bible points out that God is the "King of ages, immortal, invisible, the ONLY God" (1 Timothy 1:17; emphasis added). So when we were created in God's image, we were given the gift of uniqueness—individuality. This is reflected in the fact that God gave us a free will—the ability to choose.

When God set the first human beings in the Garden of Eden, He laid out a pretty good spread for them. They had all the food they could stand and all the animals to romp with. However, He also set in the Garden a mysterious tree called the tree of the knowledge of good and evil. And instead of nullifying humans' ability to choose and be individuals, He let them have a choice to obey or disobey His command.

> *Why do you think God would give people the ability to choose? Wouldn't things have been better if He hadn't given us the ability to be unique?*

"And the LORD God commanded the man, saying, 'You may surely eat of every tree of the garden, but of the tree of the knowledge of good and evil you shall not eat, for in the day that you eat of it you shall surely die' " (Genesis 2:16, 17).

Well, I'm sure you can guess what happened. One day Eve was meandering around, far away from Adam, when a sly snake—the devil in disguise—convinced her to eat from that tree by saying, " 'For God knows that when you eat of it your eyes will be opened, and you will be like God, knowing good and evil' " (Genesis 3:5). There are a couple of different components to this blatant lie.

God had told them that if they ate from the tree they would die (2:17). He was giving them the chance to trust and depend on Him for their happiness despite their having the ability to reject Him and do their own thing. Well, long story short, Adam and Eve had a little lunch at the forbidden tree and violated God's trust. Not to mention that the taking of the off-limits fruit was them saying, "We don't need God. We can be our own gods, just as the snake said."

So one hearty *chomp!* later and we have the world's first act of rebellion—otherwise known as the world's first sin. Humans had a chance for a perfect life serving God in the Garden, but instead we denied our dependence on Him by taking the fruit into our own hands—and that's when the problems started. When we stop depending on God, there is nothing to depend on.

A favorite trick I used to play on my siblings was to remove something they were depending on. Usually it occurred while they watched TV. One of my brothers would be lying on his side supporting his head with his hand. The trick? Yank the hand out from under the head. It would involve some patience, stealth, and some powerful quick reflexes, but the end result was always worth it. See, after one has been mindlessly viewing for ten minutes or so, one's head begins to rest more and more on the hand, and one becomes more and more oblivious to the surroundings. So when I come along and yank the hand—well, the head does one of two things.

It will either bob violently, resulting in an "OW!" as a brother stops his head at the last possible second before it hits the floor; or it will hit the floor. This also results in "OW!" but only after there is a marvelous *thump!* (Quick note: No one was ever seriously injured, just really annoyed.)

In the same way, when we stop depending on God, we lose our major support system, and the results are never good. Just look at what happened to Adam and Eve.

"Then the eyes of both were opened, and they knew that they were naked. And they sewed fig leaves together and made themselves loincloths"

(Genesis 3:7). Now I used to think this was the goofiest text in the Bible. I mean, how could you *not* know you were naked? But there is something different at work here besides modesty. When man and woman were created, the Bible says they were naked and "felt no shame" (Genesis 2:25, NIV). When they sinned, something changed. They saw themselves in their sin, they were exposed for their rebellion, and for the first time, they had something to be ashamed about.

Picture having a dream where for some reason you have managed to show up naked to class. However, you are conscious enough to know it's a dream so you say "Who cares?" and proceed to PE to play football in the buff. No big deal. It's a dream, and no one cares in the dream. But suppose in the middle of that game you suddenly wake up . . . and it's not a dream! It's actually happening. What would you do?

You'd probably run the fastest touchdown of your life and then continue running all the way home and tell your parents that while you don't know why you are naked, you *do* know that you're never ever going back to school again. Then you would probably hide under your bed. Adam and Eve felt the same way.

"And they heard the sound of the LORD God walking in the garden in the cool of the day, and the man and his wife hid themselves from the presence of the LORD God among the trees of the garden" (Genesis 3:8). A lot of people do this when they sin. They hide from God. Adam and Eve also did the other thing humans do when they mess up.

"He said, 'Who told you that you were naked? Have you eaten of the tree of which I commanded you not to eat?' The man said, 'The woman whom you gave to be with me, she gave me fruit of the tree, and I ate.' Then the LORD God said to the woman, 'What is this that you have done?' The woman said, 'The serpent deceived me, and I ate' " (Genesis 3:11–13). They played what my mother refers to as the blame game. Nobody wants to admit they were wrong. Kids and adults alike do this. We got it from our first parents—Adam and Eve. See for yourself.

> *How can we make sure that we admit our wrongs instead of hiding from them?*

The Nature of Man

"To the woman he said, 'I will surely multiply your pain in childbearing; in pain you shall bring forth children. Your desire shall be for your husband, and he shall rule over you.' And to Adam he said, 'Because you have listened to the voice of your wife and have eaten of the tree of which I commanded you, "You shall not eat of it," cursed is the ground because of you; in pain you shall eat of it all the days of your life' " (Genesis 3:16, 17).

What you just read in that text was what happened to the very first parents—the parents every human comes from—just before they had the kids that would have the kids that would have the kids—and so on—who would have you and me. The world was cursed, and that wonderful image we were made into was marred. We have all inherited that curse, our tendencies to be selfish and do the wrong thing. We all have it.

Have you ever seen a stripped screw? I have one I'm trying to work with right now on the outer casing of my computer. Every screw has a certain shape—grooves that the screwdriver fits into so a handyman wannabe like me can pretend they know what they are doing by unscrewing things and taking a clueless look inside what I just unscrewed. Well, when a screw is stripped, it means that the special grooves that make the screw work properly have been marred and worn away, so the screwdriver just spins and nothing happens.

We are all like stripped screws. The special "God-grooves" we are supposed to have are worn down because of years and years of sin in the human race. This means that instead of us working with God to do His will, we usually want to do our own thing.

For example, if you and your sister (just pretend you have one if you don't—her name is Bertha) are sitting in the kitchen, and your aunt (just pretend you have one if you don't—her name is Bertha) sets two pieces of the world's greatest chocolate in front of you and your sister. Let's say chocolate is your favorite thing in the world and one of the pieces happens to be bigger than the other. Which do you take? And even if you *didn't* take the bigger piece, you would rather have it, wouldn't you? You had to force yourself to do the nice thing, right? And it's the same in lots of areas. How do I know?

47

What We Believe

Is there anything in this world you hate doing but you have to because it's the right thing to do? Chores, anyone? Homework? Sometimes going to church when you could be sleeping-in until noon? Be honest, if there were no good parents, laws, or rights and wrongs defined in the Bible, we would all do things a lot differently. We would be selfish; it would be the natural thing to do. But thankfully God had better plans than letting the world slip into the chaos of people pursuing their own selfish passions. This is the reason I am not a rock star (among many other reasons).

When Jesus came to this world, He had one mission in mind: to find and save the lost (Luke 19:10). What does it mean to be saved? It means that Jesus would pay the penalty that humans were responsible for. He would die for us in order to restore God's image in the human race.

"For he himself is our peace, who has made us both one and has broken down in his flesh the dividing wall of hostility . . . and might reconcile us both to God in one body through the cross, thereby killing the hostility" (Ephesians 2:14, 16). There was a division between God and man, despite God's love. But when Jesus—God clothed with human skin—came here, He paid the price for us and made a way that we could be reconciled—or restored. The Bible calls it being made a "new creature" in Christ (2 Corinthians 5:17), even saying that the "old" us has passed away.

See, when we accept Jesus' sacrifice on our behalf and express a desire to follow God, He begins to transform us into His image!

"And we all, with unveiled face, beholding the glory of the Lord, are being transformed into the same image from one degree of glory to another. For this comes from the Lord who is the Spirit" (2 Corinthians 3:18).

When I accepted Christ as a teenager, I started to realize that my desire to be the "image" hanging in the walls of my room was not what God wanted for me. And as I followed Him more, He began to change my heart and reveal things to me. It was then that I began putting away the posters and such and began asking God to transform me into the unique me He has designed and wants me to be. I am happy I did for thousands of reasons. So I will leave you with the same advice my teenage girlfriend—and God—gave me.

"You were born an original; don't die a copy."

8 | The Great Controversy

The line had been drawn. The two opposing sides stood waiting for the signal.

The tension was as intense as the heat that day. Piercing stares, snarls, and an escalating anticipation were brewing as the two sides prepared for a grueling battle, a battle that would change their lives forever.

Both sides knew there would be losses; both sides knew they couldn't afford to show fear or hesitation; and both sides knew they had to push themselves beyond anything they had ever done before if they were to be victorious. The prize was so beautiful and so critical that, if it ended up in the wrong hands, shame and humiliation would follow the loser. Each side knew they couldn't show mercy because they would receive none. Each side understood the risks and some even walked away, leaving glory behind, unwilling to participate in one of the greatest battles of all time: Capture the Flag—junior high.

When I gave the signal to begin, the two sides crashed like waves breaching against rock. Shouts, laughter, cries of distress, and mockery rang throughout the air. People ran back and forth exerting every effort to tag someone out to defend the all-important prize—Frisbees. Each

What We Believe

side had two, one set red, the other blue, and the team to get them all safely on their side would emerge victorious.

My fellow pastors and I refereed; not because we're fair, but because we could keep things interesting. We made up rules as we went along. Before I gave the signal to begin, a young man had stepped over the line. I called false start, and he began the game in jail. If I got attitude, kids went to jail. If I got sassed, a kid went to jail. I even sent one kid to jail just because I could; you should have seen him in jail trying to figure out what happened. But the best part to watch was how adamantly and persistently they guarded the flags.

I saw kids dive and just catch the shoe of an opponent. One poor boy got trapped in the middle of the other team's side, and about five girls jumped him and he was left lying on the ground, twitching. One boy tried to stand on the flag. "Goal tending! You're out!" Nothing brings so much joy as teens griping about calls they have no control over, at least to me.

We had games go for ten minutes just waiting for someone to break through. But the best play came when one boy got the flag and was cornered by a girl half his size. He went one way and then the other, trying to psych her out. Bless her heart, she got so sick of trying to follow him that she stepped forward and slapped him. I mean, just clocked him a good one. He stumbled and fell over. And as a caring, nurturing pastor I did what I had to do—I called him out. Those teens lived and breathed this game, and they played with a passion to protect their flags from being stolen.

Another contest is going on right now, far larger and more serious than the most heated game of Capture the Flag. It's a war to protect God's character and to capture the hearts of men and women—and you.

"Now war arose in heaven, Michael and his angels fighting against the dragon. And the dragon and his angels fought back" (Revelation 12:7). It's a strange thought—a place as beautiful as heaven having to go through something as ugly as a war.

In the prophetic language of the Bible we are told that Michael (Jesus) fought against the dragon (the devil, a.k.a. Satan), and they both had armies of angels. Talk about an epic picture. Usually when we see heaven, it's portrayed as a place with streets of gold and happiness; we don't see dragons or evil angels (also known as demons) trying to attack God. How could something like this have happened? How did the devil get into heaven anyway? The answer is both frightening and sad.

In the book of Ezekiel—a book laden with prophetic imagery—we are given a glimpse into the history of heaven. We get to see the events that led up to this great war that's talked about in Revelation. Ezekiel records a conversation between God and the "king of Tyre," who represents the devil. And here is what God says:

> "Thus says the Lord GOD:
> "You were the signet of perfection, full of wisdom and perfect in beauty. You were in Eden, the garden of God; every precious stone was your covering, sardius, topaz, and diamond, beryl, onyx, and jasper, sapphire, emerald, and carbuncle; and crafted in gold were your settings and your engravings. On the day that you were created they were prepared. You were an anointed guardian cherub. I placed you; you were on the holy mountain of God; in the midst of the stones of fire you walked. You were blameless in your ways from the day you were created, till unrighteousness was found in you" (Ezekiel 28:12–15).

Believe it or not, this is the description of what the devil WAS.

When God created Satan, he was nothing like what he has become today. He wasn't even called Satan or the devil. He was called the Day Star or Morning Star and was made in absolute perfection. He was the pinnacle of God's creative power. His name was Lucifer, and he was incredibly beautiful—another difference from how he is portrayed today. The Bible even tells us that the devil still appears as an angel of light sometimes.

God also tells us that Lucifer was a guardian angel—*the* guardian angel. He was a superpower, top commander of the angels. He was even allotted a place on God's holy mountain. Can you imagine the honor and prestige that came with that position? He was Christ's right-hand

What We Believe

man—one of His best friends, no doubt. Does this give you a frightening glimpse into the amount of power our enemy was created with?

But then something happened in Lucifer's heart that would cause him to lose his lofty position and friendship with God. The Bible tells us that "unrighteousness" was found in him. And I'll bet it wouldn't take you too long to figure out what kind of sin can be found in a person who has been blessed with everything.

> In the abundance of your trade
> > you were filled with violence in your midst, and you sinned;
> so I cast you as a profane thing from the mountain of God,
> > and I destroyed you, O guardian cherub,
> > from the midst of the stones of fire.
> Your heart was proud because of your beauty;
> > you corrupted your wisdom for the sake of your splendor.
> I cast you to the ground (Ezekiel 28:16, 17).

God's ultimate created being began to question why he wasn't as exalted as God was. He began to notice his own beauty, his own wisdom, and he began to get jealous of Jesus and wanted to take His place. So Lucifer began to devise a plan to overthrow God's government. It was the ultimate conspiracy.

> *Do you think people are more at risk for rejecting God when they are more or less attractive and talented?*

Believing that God was not as suitable as he was to rule the universe, Lucifer began spreading the word that God's government wasn't fair. He began lying about God's character as well. We can see an echo of this in the book of Job—a story about a man blessed by God and yet subjected to a series of tests due to the devil's accusations about God.

"Then Satan answered the LORD and said, 'Does Job fear God for no reason? Have you not put a hedge around him and his house and all that he has, on every side? You have blessed the work of his hands, and his possessions have increased in the land. But stretch out your hand

and touch all that he has, and he will curse you to your face' " (Job 1:9–11).

The devil accused God of unfairness the same way here in the book of Job as he had done in heaven. *And if God isn't fair,* he reasoned, *what's keeping me from taking His place? Just look at me! I'm perfect!* Sin in the form of pride had weakened his judgment. While he may have been created in perfection, he was still created. It doesn't matter how powerful you are, nobody is tough enough to take God down.

> *Do you think tests like the one Job had still happen for followers of God? What does this tell you about suffering in the world?*

Recently I was perusing a copy of the Darwin Awards. The Darwin Awards are accounts of people doing incredibly stupid things resulting in injury or death. One story was of a macho man from Pennsylvania back in 1997. His name was Ken, and he was over at a friend's house when he reached into his friend's terrarium (an aquarium without water) to play with the pet cobra. The cobra, not excited about being picked up, bit Ken's hand and injected venom into his veins.

Now most intelligent people would race to the phone and dial 9-1-1 to get some medical attention and some anti-venom. But not Ken—no sir! Ken thought himself extremely powerful and impressive, and he refused his friend's offer to take him to the hospital by saying, "I'm a man, I can handle it."

So instead of going to the hospital, Ken visited his local bar, thinking all was well. The thing is, cobra venom is a slow-acting central nervous system toxin, and it worked slowly enough to allow Ken enough time to have three drinks while he bragged about being bitten by a snake.

Unfortunately, a few hours later, Ken succumbed to the poison and dropped dead as a reminder to all who knew him that when you are full of poison, being full of yourself is not a good idea.

In reality it was just as dumb for the devil to allow the sin of pride to poison him into thinking he could "handle" it when squaring off against God Almighty. When the battle did begin, it was short-lived. The Bible records God throwing out the devil and a third of the angels (the ones the devil had tricked using his incredible power).

Unfortunately, as they were thrown to earth they devised a way to get back at God—attack His creation. In the Garden of Eden the devil attacked mankind by using the same sin that had ensnared him. Disguising himself as a serpent, he told Adam and Even to eat from the tree God had forbidden to them by saying, "But the serpent said to the woman, 'You will not surely die. For God knows that when you eat of it your eyes will be opened, and you will be like God, knowing good and evil' " (Genesis 3:4, 5).

Satan tempted Adam and Eve with the idea that they could be like God and that God just didn't want to have any equals. And unfortunately, they listened to the talking snake. When they took the forbidden fruit, they brought the battle that had raged in heaven down here to earth. The devil thought he could prove his point that no one can truly obey God because He isn't fair—human beings were his proof. When they ate from the tree, Adam and Eve hurt their connection to God and marred the image He created them with—they were just as prone to sin as the devil was.

This called for drastic measures.

The entire universe looked on to see how God would respond to His creation falling under the domination of sin. He has worked tirelessly through the ages through miracles, signs, and special messengers; but all those were merely pointing to the greatest attack plan of all: an invasion by God Himself.

The Bible records the invasion in the birth of Jesus when it says, " 'Behold, the virgin shall conceive and bear a son, and they shall call his name Immanuel' (which means, God with us)" (Matthew 1:23). God made a personal appearance right smack in the middle of the battlefield we call earth.

Speaking of this invasion, Philip Yancey, a well-known Christian author, says, "In heaven the Great Invasion had begun, a daring raid by the ruler of the forces of good into the universe's seat of evil."* As it

---

*Philip Yancey, *The Jesus I Never Knew* (Grand Rapids: Zondervan, 2002), 43.

stands, Earth is the only planet that has sin on it; it is the battlefield of the universe, with the devil himself making it his fortress. But God loves us so much that He had to come and rescue us. So He put on human flesh, took our weaknesses, and made the most daring rescue ever recorded.

> *What risks did Jesus take by becoming a weak human being in order to save us from death?*

As we have already discussed, Jesus endured countless temptations and pains as He fought to live the perfect life of love. The devil grew angry at Christ's success, and so he lured one of Jesus' own disciples—Judas—into betraying Him to His death. However, despite the cruelty and agony Jesus went through, His death provided the forgiveness from sin we needed and the way to rejoin God's side. Christ's invasion took away our sin and vindicated God before the universe. Jesus proved that God could be obeyed and that He was loving and fair.

While Jesus was successful on the cross, there is still a work to be done. The war is not completely over yet. "So Christ was sacrificed once to take away the sins of many people; and he will appear a second time, not to bear sin, but to bring salvation to those who are waiting for him" (Hebrews 9:28, NIV). People needed and still need to know what Jesus did for them. Then there will be a Second Invasion, and Jesus will take His followers home to be with Him. This is the part of the war being fought now—the one for the human heart.

"For we do not wrestle against flesh and blood, but against the rulers, against the authorities, against the cosmic powers over this present darkness, against the spiritual forces of evil in the heavenly places" (Ephesians 6:12).

The Bible makes it clear the devil's forces—although ultimately defeated on the cross—are still causing trouble in the world. There are murders, abuse, starvation, natural disasters, doubts, and false religions, just to name a few of the enemy's weapons.

Why do you think the devil is still fighting against men and God, even though he has already been proven wrong on the cross? One reason is that he is trying to take down as many people as he can—just as

What We Believe

he took a third of the angels with him when he was cast out of heaven. God loves us so much that the thought of losing even one of us hurts Him deeply. The devil, by preventing people from hearing the message of Jesus or receiving Him as their Savior, keeps men and women in darkness and hurts God. And he does it with everything he's got.

> *What other weapons do you think the devil uses to keep human beings in the darkness?*

This means you and I need to be sure we keep our relationship with God connected and strong. Our enemy is just waiting for a chance to trap us. Thankfully, God has promised us His power if we ask for it; and He has also promised us power when we are trying to remove the darkness around our friends and family who don't know Jesus yet.

Eventually this war will be brought to a close. Just as Revelation talks of the war in heaven, it also mentions the Second Invasion. At the second coming of Jesus, in which God's enemies will be destroyed once and for all, we will be taken to a new home where war will never happen again.

There is still a lot at stake. Forces of good and evil are battling for mankind and its future; even one loss is too many. But God has promised that there will be victory when He returns, and we can rest assured that while battles still rage, He has already won the war. Let's keep that hope before us every day as we fight alongside God's angels, helping them capture the hearts of men and women for Jesus.

9 | The Life, Death, and Resurrection of Jesus

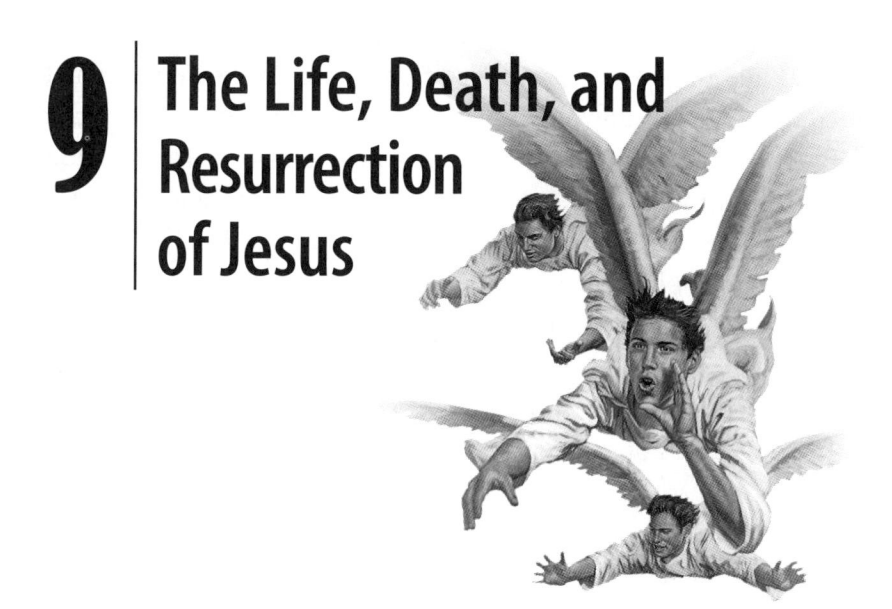

Last year I picked up what looked like a really exciting book about a man who made a great contribution to the world. His name was Ferdinand Magellan, and he was the first person to circumnavigate the globe back in the days when they had only wooden ships and no global positioning systems.

The book promised exciting adventures, pirates, wicked storms, and all sorts of crazy stuff that would make for an exciting read—especially because it was all true! I dove into the book, and sure enough, it was packed full of excitement. I read how Magellan avoided a mutiny when four of his five ships were taken over by unhappy sailors, and how his crew was attacked by islanders, who were more interested in eating Magellan's crew than greeting them. It was exciting to see how Magellan navigated his way through areas of the world that were perilous to travel by boat.

But I hit a snag three-quarters of the way through. What was the snag? He died. Before he finished his trip.

It was so depressing. I had always thought Magellan made it. The worst part was how he died. He brazenly attacked some islanders in the Philippines in a battle he shouldn't have fought. He was shot with poison arrows and hacked to pieces in a battle he engaged in because of his own pride. The book makes the comment, "His loyalists believed he had courted death by picking an unnecessary quarrel."*

While the book was still good and I would recommend it, I must confess I was let down by Magellan. And as I've since taken up reading biographies of the most fascinating people from spiritual leaders like Martin Luther to pirates like Captain Kidd, I am disappointed at what I see in the lives of these famous (or infamous) people. Nobody lives up to the hype. Nobody is perfect.

Even in the Bible we can see great leaders messing up. Moses was a murderer; Noah got drunk and lost his clothes; and all of the disciples fell asleep when they should have been praying. Everywhere you look, from your pastor to your parents—people mess things up. No one is perfect. Except One—Jesus Christ.

"But we have one who has been tempted in every way, just as we are—yet was without sin" (Hebrews 4:15, NIV). Jesus Christ came to this world with the mission to find and save the people who didn't know God loved them. That verse says He encountered temptation (or situations that would make you want to do something wrong) and He refused to give in. Can you imagine having the mission to express love to people—every second of your life—and you were harassed by evil behavior left and right? I can't.

I mean, I get mad every day when I'm cut off in traffic, or I get stressed out because I have so much homework to do, or because life presents me with hard decisions. Jesus was mocked (Luke 23:36), plotted against (John 11:53), beaten and spit on (Luke 18:32), and even killed (John 19:30). Even while He was hanging from iron nails through His hands and feet He didn't sin. To be honest, if I were being tortured to death, I'd probably have a few choice things to say or at least think about those hurting me. But Jesus said, " 'Father, forgive them, for they do not know what they are doing' " (Luke 23:34, NIV). How could He do that? What would make someone willing to go through torture and death while refusing to sin?

" 'For God so loved the world, that he gave his only Son, that whoever believes in him should not perish but have eternal life' " (John 3:16).

What is perhaps the most famous Bible text in the Bible tells us that

---

*Laurence Bergreen, *Over the Edge of the World* (New York: Harper Perennial, 2004), 284.

because God loves us so much, He sent us Jesus to tell us about it and to prove it in His life—and His death. But why go to all that trouble? Wouldn't a greeting card have been good enough? Is there a reason Jesus had to come to earth and die? And how does it relate to eternal life?

When you have credit cards—and you use them—it is a good thing to pay them off. That's what I was trying to do when I sent my bank a fifteen hundred dollar payment for some purchases I made a couple months before. I got online, accessed my account, and after punching in some numbers I clicked the Submit button and sent my payment off into cyberspace. One month later, when I saw my account statement, those fifteen hundred dollars had not shown up, and I was being fined with a late charge. I was *not* happy.

I went to the bank in person to share what was on my heart (fiery rage) and to see if I couldn't get them to find my money. After bumbling around for a while they told me they couldn't find it and asked if I had really paid my bill. Normally, a situation like this would cause a person to panic as fifteen hundred buckaroos hardly qualifies as pocket change. But thankfully I had something with me that vindicated me and pointed to the bank as the one that had made the mistake.

See, after I submitted my online payment, I printed my receipt and confirmation number. Kids, listen to me here—PRINT YOUR RECEIPTS! Or at least save them. I had them as proof.

I slapped down that piece of paper on the counter with great gusto and said, "Take a look at this and tell me what you see." They took a look—and they weren't happy.

"Just a second," they grumbled.

Long story short, they took off the fines and paid off my credit card. There was nothing they could do against an official receipt. I was vindicated, and my account was restored.

When the devil rebelled in heaven and was cast out, one of the biggest accusations he had was that God's way of doing things was not fair. As we saw in the last chapter, the devil went so far as to try to remove God in a battle. Then, when he was thrown to earth, he brought his rebellious nature with him and tempted Adam and Eve to fall to sin in the Garden of Eden—thereby thinking he had proven once and for all that God's ways could not be followed. If the devil had been right he would have doomed mankind, because the penalty for sin is death (look up Romans 6:23). And he would have proven that God cannot be followed.

Enter Jesus.

"For to this you have been called, because Christ also suffered for you, leaving you an example, so that you might follow in his steps. He committed no sin, neither was deceit found in his mouth" (1 Peter 2:21, 22).

Jesus is God's—and our—receipt of payment for the whole universe to see. He came and lived the perfect life we should have lived, died in our place, and proved that God's ways are fair and livable. Through His life and death He vindicated us and God, which means the devil is a liar and he has lost. But Christ's tremendous life, which is the most fascinating biography of all, didn't end with His death.

The Bible says, "concerning his Son, who was descended from David according to the flesh and was declared to be the Son of God in power according to the Spirit of holiness by his resurrection from the dead, Jesus Christ our Lord" (Romans 1:3, 4). Jesus was so powerful that He rose from the dead. No biography in history save this one ends like that.

When He rose from the dead He challenged His followers to do their best in living a life just like His, and He would be there through His Spirit to help them. "Therefore, we are ambassadors for Christ, God making his appeal through us. We implore you on behalf of Christ, be reconciled to God. For our sake he made him to be sin who knew no sin, so that in him we might become the righteousness of God" (2 Corinthians 5:20, 21).

How do you think Jesus could make your life different than it is now?

We are challenged to be Christ's representatives on earth. We are challenged to live a life just like Jesus. How does that affect the way you think of your life? For me, it's exciting because it means that the Person living the greatest existence ever is leading and guiding my life. The Lord of Life is in charge of mine. And while I can never live in a way that makes as big an impact as Christ's, He can shape my life and yours into a wonderful story, a biography that will not end in a disappointing death.

10 | The Experience of Salvation

A couple of months ago my wife and I were sitting on our bed watching television and eating supper. Angela had made her famous and ridiculously delicious lentils with melted cheese on top just like I like it. After relishing supper we set our bowls aside on the bedspread and continued watching our show—waiting for a commercial break to take our dishes back to the sink. That's when my cat Wahpeton came on the scene.

Wahpeton is gray and white and very sweet. However, I've always suspected that Wahpeton is a few scoops short of a full litter box. That evening he gave me further cause for concern. He jumped on the bed and, instead of sitting by our side or meowing for attention, he began pawing at the white comforter.

"Ha!" cried my wife. "Look at your cat—what's he doing?"

At first I wasn't sure what to think of it. He would paw at it with one paw, and then when that paw got tired, he would paw at it with the other. He did this for a good two or three minutes. Eventually it dawned on us that he was trying to dig, which made Angela laugh and me shake my head. I mean, it was so embarrassing. You'd think Wahpeton would get it after a while that he was *not* digging in dirt. Just as I was about to call the kitty psychiatrist, he stopped. Not on his own, mind you. When Angela took away the bowls we had been eating our food from, the answer to my cat's mysterious digging dawned on us, making me laugh—and my wife scowl.

"My cooking is a lot better than—!"

"Now, dear, he doesn't know any better. He's only a cat. He doesn't eat people food."

"It doesn't matter! I can't believe he thinks my food is—"

"Well, I thought it was good, and that's all that matters!"

Cats are very tidy animals, and they are particular about how and where they . . . uh . . . do their business. And when they . . . uh . . . make a business transaction, they bury it in their litter box or in the yard. They are private that way. And when Wahpeton smelled the smell of people food, he mistook it for . . . uh . . . something unpleasant. Hence, he was doing his utmost to bury it, even though there was no dirt.

It wouldn't have mattered if he dug for three years, he wouldn't have found the way to bury the bowl. It was only when it was taken away from him that he stopped—free of something that was apparently very unpleasing to him. Only his master—me—could save him from that stuff which made his life unpleasant.

Jesus did the same thing for us with sin. We all know we make mistakes and aren't perfect, and yet, despite our own diligent efforts, we can never remove it from our lives. We need help to remove the stinking substance of sin from our lives, so Jesus (our Master) provided that help.

John 3:16 tells us that God loved us so much that He sent His Son to remove our sins by dying in our place. And God told us that if we just believe in Christ we will have eternal life. By coming here and living the life He did, Jesus removed our sins and made us right with God. "How much more will the blood of Christ, who through the eternal Spirit offered himself without blemish to God, purify our conscience from dead works to serve the living God" (Hebrews 9:14). And not only did God remove the sin from our lives, but He offers it as a free gift to anyone who will accept it. That's grace.

The Experience of Salvation

But even though we are offered the free removal of sin from our lives, a good relationship with God and a place in heaven, a lot of people don't understand how to receive it. They don't know how to take it for themselves. They study it, talk about it, speculate about it, and try to judge who is and who isn't saved. But in reality, salvation in Jesus Christ must be experienced.

> *Why and how do you think people try to get salvation on their own?*

Think about it. How valuable is experience? If you were going to have brain surgery, would you want the doctor with the most or the least experience? If you had the option of going to Hawaii or just reading about it, which would you choose? If you could have the power to actually fly or just dream about having the power to fly, which would you rather have? Yeah, I thought so. Experience is important. Yet I am amazed at how many people don't have an experience with Jesus.

Whenever I give someone a Bible study, the first question I ask *before* we study is, "Do you know Jesus as your Friend and Savior?" Nearly all the time I get a blank stare. So I ask again, rephrasing it. "Do you feel like you know Jesus personally?" Again a blank stare. They don't know. They may know a lot about Christianity, what Jesus did, and what it's like to be in church, but they have never formally accepted Jesus Christ as their Savior, telling Him their sins, and asking Him to lead and guide everything they do in life. And acting like a Christian without knowing Jesus personally is simply being religious, and that can be dangerous.

The Bible has a nifty little story about a group of guys known as the Seven Sons of Sceva, who ran into some trouble with a nasty demon. They were all the sons of a high priest named—that's right—Sceva. They had all seen Paul do some amazing things because he had a personal relationship with Jesus. One of those things was casting out demons that had taken control of people's lives. It looked like fun, so the Seven Sons of Sceva gave it a whirl. The only problem was that they didn't have an experience with Jesus. They just knew He was a friend of Paul. And, well, look what happened.

What We Believe

And God was doing extraordinary miracles by the hands of Paul, so that even handkerchiefs or aprons that had touched his skin were carried away to the sick, and their diseases left them and the evil spirits came out of them. Then some of the itinerant Jewish exorcists undertook to invoke the name of the Lord Jesus over those who had evil spirits, saying, "I adjure you by the Jesus, whom Paul proclaims." Seven sons of a Jewish high priest named Sceva were doing this. But the evil spirit answered them, "Jesus I know, and Paul I recognize, but who are you?" And the man in whom was the evil spirit leaped on them, mastered all of them and overpowered them, so that they fled out of that house naked and wounded. And this became known to all the residents of Ephesus, both Jews and Greeks. And fear fell upon them all, and the name of the Lord Jesus was extolled (Acts 19:11–17).

Wow. The demon recognized Paul because Paul belonged to Jesus—Paul had a personal experience with Jesus, a real friendship. The Seven Sons of Sceva did not, and they got a whupping. There is no substituting being religious for having a personal experience with Jesus. True victory over sin and the devil demands that we have one. Not to mention it is the most powerful tool for sharing God's love with the rest of the world.

Studies show that the most effective advertising is word of mouth. Think about it. If you are looking for a good book, you are more likely to go for the one your best friend has been raving about versus the one you know nothing about. Or if you wanted to find a good deal on, well, anything, you might go to people you know who have what it is you're looking for and ask them about where they got theirs.

When I was in Peru for a short-term mission trip, we were served a variety of foreign foods we had never tried before. One such food was a little fruit that reminded me of a kiwi. However, inside it looked like snotty boogers. I'm fully aware of how gross that sounds, but that is the only way to describe it. So you can imagine when we were shown this despicable-looking delicacy that we were reluctant to try it. Eventually someone agreed to be the guinea pig and give it a try.

We watched as he slurped out the slimy green guts and dark seeds. We stared intently just waiting for him to keel over or throw up. But that didn't happen. As a matter of fact he began nodding his head and smiling.

"It's good! It tastes good!"

Based on that recommendation, we all picked up one of the fruits and, after hesitating just a little, sucked out its innards. It was good. It tasted like a combination of a kiwi, banana, and strawberry. And we never would have tried it had we not had a recommendation—a testimony—from someone we knew who told us how good it was.

"That which was from the beginning, which we have heard, which we have seen *with our eyes,* which we looked upon and have touched with our hands, *concerning the word of life—the life was made manifest,* and we have seen it, and testify to it *and proclaim to you the eternal life, which was with the Father and was made manifest to us—that which we have seen and heard we proclaim also to you, so that you too may have fellowship with us; and indeed our fellowship is with the Father and with his Son Jesus Christ"* (1 John 1:1–3; emphasis added).

If John wanted to condense this part of his book all he would have to say is "That which we have experienced." Jesus' follower John made sure people knew that when he talked about faith and Jesus, it was birthed out of his personal experience. And as a result of Jesus' followers' personal experiences with Him, they were able to spread the gospel everywhere. But even with our testimony there is no substitute for inviting the person listening to us to experience the same joy.

Have you ever told one of those jokes or one of those stories where no one seems to get what you're talking about and you have to end it by saying, "You just had to be there"? It is hard to explain some things when people haven't actually experienced them.

Can you imagine trying to describe a hug if you had never received one? You could tell people what it involves; but could you really express the warmth and love that goes along with it? And could you imagine telling someone about the view on top of a mountain when you've never been there? You might be able to say the specific things you've seen, but to express the majesty and grandeur of the sight, well, they'd just have to be there.

Salvation is the same way. In order to really share what it's like with someone, you need to experience it yourself. A lot of Christians have painted their faith very poorly for people because they didn't have a genuine positive experience with Jesus. And even when you do have the experience of salvation, words fail to describe how great it is. It is kind of like describing the color blue to someone who has been blind their entire life. Words alone just won't work. You need experience.

Experience with Jesus gives you something to talk about to the people in your life who might not know Jesus. They might be skeptical or doubting, but they will find it hard to argue when you passionately share what Jesus has done to change your life. They may even begin asking how they can have the same experience as you. And that's when they will truly understand the beauty of the salvation experience.

So let me ask you the question: Do you know Jesus? Have you said a prayer to officially ask Him to come into your life, forgive your sins, and guide your life? Being religious won't remove your sins and change your life. Only a personal saving relationship chock full of experiences can do that. Why don't you take time right now to reflect on your life and ask yourself if you have personally experienced the salvation Jesus gives or if you have simply been religious? And if you have only been religious, why not ask Jesus to give you the experience of salvation? It will change your life and change the lives of others as you share your experience with them.

11 | Growing in Christ

In first grade I was given one of the most tremendous assignments of my life. It was an assignment on the very cutting edge of science. I was given state-of-the-art equipment and highly detailed instructions in order to fulfill my purpose. The equipment consisted of a cup, some soil, and one bean. The mission?

Grow the bean.

Yeah, I know it's pitiful, but I gave it all I had. I did the whole watering and sunshine thing in hopes of producing one solitary bean plant and thereby producing an A on my report card. They were tense times. Every day I went to check my project, and every day I was greeted with the same cup of lifeless soil . . . until one day there was a breakthrough.

Like a mad scientist hovering over his creation I greedily stared at the little Styrofoam cup that now contained a little bean sprout reaching toward the heavens (my bedroom ceiling). It was one of the better successes of my science career; actually it was one of very few successes in my science career. I can't tell you how many plants I've killed, maimed, or damaged psychologically since then. But my bean was so exciting!

What We Believe

Growth and improvement are always exciting—especially when it comes to our relationship with Jesus. Yes, Jesus gives us an assignment to grow. He tells us that whoever has a relationship with Him will demonstrate powerful things in their life. Jesus called it "bearing fruit."

When Jesus was chatting with His disciples about having a relationship with Him, He used an analogy of being a branch grafted into a vine.

" 'Abide in me, and I in you. As the branch cannot bear fruit by itself, unless it abides in the vine, neither can you, unless you abide in me. I am the vine; you are the branches. Whoever abides in me and I in him, he it is that bears much fruit, for apart from me you can do nothing. If anyone does not abide in me he is thrown away like a branch and withers; and the branches are gathered, thrown into the fire, and burned' " (John 15:4–6).

Grafting is a cool process used in agriculture and medicine. The basic concept of agricultural grafting is taking a branch of one tree and attaching it to another. You make a cut into the tree, and the branch is attached into the groove, and then they're tied together. Eventually they grow together, and the branch will bud leaves and even grow fruit. I have seen pictures of multiple branches grafted—or "abiding"—in a tree to form crazy diamond patterns in the trunk for artistic purposes. It's really amazing to look at.

Why is Jesus so serious about people growing in their relationship with Him? What is the reason we are supposed to become more like Jesus? Isn't accepting Him enough?

In medicine, an area of skin is taken from one part of the body and used to cover up a wound or surgical cut in another part of the body. After a while the skin becomes attached and grows into the place where it was grafted—it's amazing stuff. And what is even more amazing: Jesus tells us that we can be grafted into Him. We can be grown into the same power (frequently referred to as the "divine nature") as He has. Actually, He expects it.

Growing in Christ

Jesus goes so far as to say that people who don't grow in their relationship with Him will be "cut off" and "thrown out." Growth is really important to Jesus; and we must "abide" in Him if we are going to do it, because within ourselves we don't have the power.

One cruel trick I loved to play on my siblings was something I did when they were pouring their hearts into a video game. They would be furiously tapping buttons, doing their utmost to save the world, or at least to save themselves from dying and having to start the game over.

In the middle of their heated gaming frenzy I would do a run-by unplugging of the controller. It took great speed and precision, but the results were always worth it. By unplugging their controller, I unplugged their power. And when they had no power, their character on screen was rendered paralyzed. The reaction was priceless.

At first—after I had unplugged their controller—they would do a few involuntary "dry taps" on the controller. *Tap-tap-tap-tap* . . . nothing.

By this time they realized something was wrong and began to panic. "What's wrong with this thing?" they would exclaim. It didn't take long before . . .

"My controller! How did—? Seth!"

By this time I was laughing and running away from them as they were left with a frustrating choice. They could either run after me to give me the justice I probably deserved at the expense of losing their game. Or they could plug in their controller, reestablishing power, and save their game, but then I would get away for sure. It was really a delightful plan.

Just as you need to be plugged in with your controller to play a video game, you need to "abide" in a relationship with Christ in order to live the life of growth that He wants for you. After all, the Bible says that apart from Christ we can't do anything. So how do we get plugged in?

Perhaps the most important part of a Christian's life—besides believing in Jesus—is devotional time with God. A devotional life simply means the part of your day that you "devote" to God. See, if your relationship with Jesus was a bean, your devotional life would be the equivalent to sunshine, water, and fertilizer—fertilizer that doesn't stink. I wish I could tell you just exactly what your devotional life should be like, but I can't, because no two look the same. But the Bible does give us a few tips on what to include.

"Devote yourselves to prayer, being watchful and thankful" (Colossians 4:2, NIV). A famous preacher named D. L. Moody once said, "Every great movement of God can be traced to a kneeling figure." If we want to see God move in our lives, a primary part of our devotional time needs to be spent in prayer. We can be honest with God about our struggles and praise Him for our victories. We can talk to Him about whatever we are feeling inside and don't have to fake being religious with Him. He knows what's going on inside anyway.

"Do your best to present yourself to God as one approved, a worker who has no need to be ashamed, rightly handling the word of truth" (2 Timothy 2:15). As I write this I have just finished an atrocious final test as I study to attain my master's degree. It took two hours of solid writing and an entire day to study for—that means about ten hours of doing nothing but reviewing the subject. You can imagine the fun I had. However, all that study paid off when I got to the test and actually had answers to write down. I saw several people leave the test early on, having run out of things to say, and I was thankful I did enough work to be able to pass the test. We are encouraged to study God's Word—you know, the Book containing the best advice and instructions you could ever hope to have. And part of studying is being willing to apply it to your life and do what it says as well. As a result we will get a deeper understanding of God's will for our lives and what His plans are for us.

"But his delight is in the law of the Lord, and on his law he meditates day and night" (Psalm 1:2). Now by meditation this doesn't mean sitting in a lotus position and chanting "ohm"; it means simply letting the Word of God roll around in your mind throughout the day. It means taking the verse(s) you read and looking at them every way you can with your mind's eye. This is a way of listening to God. Too many times when we talk to people we are thinking about what we are going to say as soon as they get done talking to us. We do the same thing with God if we spend a brief moment or two looking at His Word and then race on to something else and don't hear everything He wants to say to us. When we take time to think about God's Word, He can reveal how He wants us to implement what we've read into our lives.

Prayer, time in God's Word, and meditation are all key parts of growing your relationship with Jesus with the hope of producing fruit. But what exactly does spiritual fruit look like? It's not like you can buy it at Wal-Mart or pick it off a tree. Thankfully the Bible has it covered.

"But the fruit of the Spirit is love, joy, peace, patience, kindness, goodness, faithfulness, gentleness, self-control; against such things there is no law" (Galatians 5:22, 23). When someone is growing in Christ, they tend to exhibit the traits listed in these verses. Another way to look at this is that we will become more and more like Jesus—who exemplified all of these qualities in His life. This doesn't mean that we will never struggle with these things. We just need to be honest about what areas we need to grow in and then ask God to help us as we study and meditate on His Word, to help us demonstrate the "fruit of the Spirit."

Do you think people are ever resistant to growing in their relationship with Jesus?

Growing isn't always easy. Sometimes we have to be more patient than we'd like, staring at the soil of our life, waiting for some sign of our spiritual life to emerge. But if we keep nurturing our relationship with Jesus through our devotional life, we will accomplish the most important assignment we have ever been given, to "grow in the grace and knowledge of our Lord and Savior Jesus Christ" (2 Peter 3:18). In other words, to grow to be more like Jesus.

12 | The Church

If someone asked you to define the word *church*, what would you tell them? How would you describe it? Some people would say church is a pointy building with crosses, pews, and dusty hymnals. Others would say it was a denomination like Adventist, Baptist, or Unitarian. And still others might say that church is just another organized religion no different from many others. What would *you* say?

If you said any of these examples, you would be partially correct because God's church is much more than a building, a denomination, or a religion.

When my wife and I were looking for an apartment a few years ago, I stumbled upon an ad for a place that looked like a little slice of heaven. The ad boasted spacious living quarters, nice grounds, and a terrific location—but those weren't the reasons I was drawn to this virtual paradise in an apartment complex. It was the amenities.

The ad boasted a dining hall that provided home-cooked, delicious meals that could be personalized upon request. This place also offered tremendous recreational activities planned out by a caring and loving staff. They had tennis tournaments, shuffleboard, square dancing, and bingo, just to name a few! It appeared to me that the people residing in this place were truly living the good life—and I wanted in.

With exuberance I showed my wife the promising ad, saying, "Honey, just look at this place! Look at all the activities they have—and they even cook your meals!" Angela took one look at the ad and then looked at me with a look only a wife can muster when she thinks her husband has lost his mind.

"It's a retirement community. You want to move to an apartment for the elderly?"

"Dear, just think about it! Cooked meals? Planned activities? And it would be so quiet!" I said, smiling.

"No."

"Oh, come on! Just consider it. Monday nights we could play bingo; then Tuesday nights we could—"

"No."

"Why not? We could dominate everyone in sports, and—"

"No."

"Please?"

"Um . . . no."

"Fine."

So we ended up moving into an apartment with a nice fireplace, vaulted ceilings, and an outdoor pool. But it was missing one thing the retirement home had—community.

It's not that we didn't occasionally have friends or a neighbor over once in a while on the weekends. But when our guests left, we remained in an apartment building that was not interested in community—or even bingo. People were friendly; they just didn't get together like the residents of the retirement complex. People visited and got together on weekends, but everyone did their own thing during the week. No activities, no cooking staff to make meals for us and our neighbors, and no midweek shuffleboard contests.

It reminds me of the limited ideas people have of church sometimes. For a lot of people church is just a nice building where people visit for a couple of hours on the weekend. But God has always had bigger plans

What We Believe

for His church than simply being a weekend worship facility. God's church isn't a building. As a matter of fact, one of the first times the Bible mentions God's "congregation" (or church) is in reference to a group of people rather than to their facility.

"Moses assembled all the congregation of the people of Israel and said to them, 'These are the things that the Lord has commanded you to do'" (Exodus 35:1). Actually the word used here for congregation simply means "a gathering" or a group of people. What's interesting to note is that this group of people were all enmeshed together traveling across the wilderness into the Promised Land God was going to give them (look up Exodus 12:25). They spent their lives together every day—not just a couple of hours on the weekends. In other words, they were a community of people who were following the words God had given to them. God's congregation not only shared life, but they shared it in a way that expressed God's love to each other and those they came in contact with.

In 1903, Bernarr Macfadden created an organization in Coney Island, New York, known as the Polar Bear Club. It was his belief that a dip in the ocean during the winter can be a boon to one's stamina, virility, and immunity. That's right, friends, a dip in the ocean in the winter in the *northeastern* part of the United States. No, I'm not making this up.

Their season begins in October and runs throughout the winter, with water temperatures being an average thirty-three degrees Fahrenheit. That's cold. If you want to see just how cold that is, watch the Weather Channel, and when it tells you that it's thirty-three degrees, go stand outside in your swimming suit.

Now imagine that you heard about this organization from a friend or a flyer but had no idea what they did. You just like polar bears and thought that this is maybe a club where they raise them, visit them at the zoo, or cuddle stuffed animal versions of them. But as soon as you join up, they slap a swimsuit on you and toss you into freezing ocean water. Would you come back for more?

Sometimes the church is like the Polar Bear Club when it comes to how people relate to each other. Not that congregations typically throw

The Church

people in cold ocean water, unless you count being baptized in cold water when the water heater breaks. But sometimes they are less than warm when they interact with people, especially new people. It might be a look, a gesture, or an unkind word—but sometimes the church just isn't friendly.

I was told by a teacher that when he first joined the church he was really excited and fired up for Jesus. When he came to church he expressed to some of the people who had been there longer than he had all sorts of great ideas for expressing God's love to people. One gentleman came up to him, put his hand on his shoulder and said, "Son, you are just excited because you're new—just give it time and you'll lose it like everyone else." Talk about a cold, wet blanket. God never designed for His community to be unloving and not excited about sharing God's love with the world.

Take a look at what the church was like right after Jesus went back up to heaven and sent the Holy Spirit. The Bible says, "There was not a needy person among them, for as many as were owners of lands or houses sold them and brought the proceeds of what was sold and laid it at the apostles' feet, and it was distributed to each as any had need" (Acts 4:34, 35). Each member of God's loving community gave up what they had to make sure that no one lacked anything. Imagine a group of people that welcomed everyone and went out of their way to include everyone in their activities *and* made sure that nobody ever was in need because they were willing to give what they had to make sure everyone was provided for.

In addition to being a community of people following God and sharing His love with each other, God has given His church a special mission—although sometimes they don't accept it.

A while ago I was working with some kids from the community, and I was excited because some wanted to attend church and have some social events during the evenings. This church was small and really hadn't had young people for a long time. So when I brought my suggestion to have the youth come to church, the idea was thrown out because the people on the board felt as though kids from the "world" would just bring a mess into the church. They thought the kids were too "into the

What We Believe

world" (even though they had never met them), and so they had to be left out of the church. I had to go pray before I hurt someone, I was so angry.

The Bible tells us God's community is a "chosen race, a royal priesthood, a holy nation, a people for his own possession, that you may proclaim the excellencies of him who called you out of darkness into his marvelous light" (1 Peter 2:9). Some Christians feel that because God's church is holy and special, it is also exclusive—only letting in perfect people. This idea comes from a misunderstanding of what it means to be holy, which means "set apart."

> *How do churches lose their mission and sense of community?*

Take a look at this letter to Christians from James, one of Jesus' followers (who also happened to be His brother). "You adulterous people! Do you not know that friendship with the world is enmity with God? Therefore whoever wishes to be a friend of the world makes himself an enemy of God" (James 4:4). The world is at odds with God. As a matter of fact, 1 John says, "Do not love the world or the things in the world. If anyone loves the world, the love of the Father is not in him" (1 John 2:15). But in these texts "loving the world" doesn't mean that we are to run away from people who aren't in the church; you'd have to move to another planet to totally pull that off. What these texts refer to is the value system that the world holds up. It is typically very different from God's.

God's church is a community of loving people who have been called out of the darkness of the world themselves. The church consists of people who were and are willing to go against the world's culture by living a life characterized by following Jesus rather than themselves. The mission of the church is to " 'Go . . . and make disciples of all nations, baptizing them in the name of the Father and of the Son and of the Holy Spirit' " (Matthew 28:19), to " 'Go into all the world and proclaim the gospel to the whole creation' " (Mark 16:15). Jesus Himself, the Man in charge of the church (check Ephesians 5:23), told the church community to go into the world and share God's love and serve everyone they encounter, both those in the world and those in the church.

The Church

My prayer is that as you study and become a part of God's church you will strive to make it a loving community that shares life all week long—not just on weekends; and that you take up the mission given to us by Jesus to go into the world and share His love with people, giving them the right idea of what church really is—a community of people who share their lives and love with each other as they worship and follow God.

13 | The Remnant and Its Mission

Picture yourself out to dinner at the world's fanciest restaurant with your own personal hero. It doesn't matter if it's a Bible hero, a celebrity you admire, or a sports figure that impresses you—this is the person whose life inspires yours. The restaurant is grand, and everything is polished and gleaming. A live band plays your favorite music, and your heart is about ready to break through your ribcage because it's beating so hard with excitement. You've had a good hair day for once, your outfit cost a fortune, and due to a rigorous tooth brushing that has nearly worn your teeth down to nothing, your breath smells so good that people have been asking you to breathe on them all day.

You stare across the table into the face of [insert favorite hero here], and they smile back at you—it's a smile that validates your existence. Your hero has acknowledged your presence, and you can die happy. Then they ask you if you're having a good time and to tell them a little bit about yourself, which makes you so excited you choke on your own spit and have to pull away for a drink of water and a few good hacks and heaves before resuming this special moment. Your hero not only cares how your evening is going, but they are interested in your story!

You spend the next five minutes stuttering through your childhood at mach ten, which causes your mouth to run dry, so you gulp your water, which in turn causes you to hiccup through the rest of the story. You're nearly breathless as you try to wrap your mind around the fact that [inspiring hero] is giving you their undivided attention.

Your waiter arrives to take your order. You peruse the costly menu to find a worthy selection. Something impressive—but not too impressive, because you would hate to offend your special date by ordering the most expensive item on the list. After a moment you find a delicious dish that demonstrates the kind of sophisticated taste buds your date would expect you to have. However, as you open your mouth to order, [magnificent hero] cuts you off and says,

"They'll just have leftovers."

"Pardon?" says the waiter.

"What?" you say, sensing all your star-struck feelings hardening into a tight little ball of anger.

"That's right," continues [potentially deranged hero]. "Any mashed potatoes, green beans, or entrees you have leftover from last night's customers will be fine." By this point you are fuming with anger, and your waiter is trying to make sense of the situation. Seeing you both upset, [hero who could take a flying leap off a building for all you care] says, "Oh, all right, we can just wait for another table to finish, and we can just clean up the remnants they have left."

Leftovers. Remnants. These words are probably the least appetizing of all the culinary terms in the world. When asking for dinner, who in their right mind salivates over last night's leftover loaf? And it's not limited to food. Leftover clothes from an older sibling; remains after a big sale at your favorite store that you missed; and what about being picked for teams in PE?

When I had PE—something I miss dearly—we lined up to play games with two team captains who would take turns picking who they wanted until there would be one uncoordinated soul leftover. The remnant. And it was *not* a position you wanted to be in. The last one left. The one separate from the group. And yet Jesus says something very strange regarding leftovers—the last ones left.

" 'So the last [the leftovers] will be first, and the first will be last' " (Matthew 20:16, NIV). In His ministry Jesus constantly elevated and worked with the "leftovers" of society. Lepers, tax collectors, the Samaritans, the simple, and the sinners all found healing and restoration in Jesus. He loved the remnants who cried out to Him as they tried to survive in a harsh world. And even in the Old Testament, it is evident that God had remnants on His mind.

Throughout the Old Testament there are references to "remnant," and whenever they are linked with God, it's always referring to a special people God kept alive amidst turmoil in the world.

In Genesis 45, God used a series of circumstances (treachery, slavery, imprisonment—all sorts of good stuff) to bring one of His people into a position of power in Egypt. The reason was that in a few years the Middle East would have a horrible famine with no food available. It would have been the end for God's people. But Joseph—the man God brought into Egypt—had access to food in that wealthy land, and he shared it with his family who didn't live in Egypt. The reason? Well, Joseph himself explains, " 'God sent me before you to preserve for you a remnant on earth, and to keep alive for you many survivors' " (Genesis 45:7).

Remnant also referred to those who remained faithful to God despite the world around them being faithless. One of the most trying experiences for God's people in the Old Testament was when the people of Israel were taken captive by the army of Babylon because they had not listened to God. Babylon was a place where the religions stood in direct contrast to God. The people worshiped other gods and images and tried to force Israel to do the same. Amidst this horrible captivity God made promises such as:

> In that day the Lord will extend his hand yet a second time to recover the remnant that remains of his people, from Assyria, from Egypt, from Pathros, from Cush, from Elam, from Shinar,

from Hamath, and from the coastlands of the sea (Isaiah 11:11).

"Then I will gather the remnant of my flock out of all the countries where I have driven them, and I will bring them back to their fold, and they shall be fruitful and multiply" (Jeremiah 23:3).

And even when the word *remnant* itself isn't mentioned we can see the concept at work. Remember Noah? He and his family were the only ones faithful to God in the entire world, and as a result, his family was the only one spared at the great Flood by a big God-designed boat in the shape of a box. Hence, they were a remnant, the leftovers, the people whom God kept alive because they kept alive their relationship with Him.

There is even a story within the Babylonian captivity about King Nebuchadnezzar attempting to force everyone to worship a giant gold image (think a one-hundred-foot-tall version of what they hand out at the Oscar Awards) he created (look up Daniel 3). Everyone worshiped except three of God's people, who would rather die by being burned alive than worship an image—literally. They were thrown into a fiery furnace so hot it killed the people throwing them in. However, Jesus appeared in the flames with them—much to the astonishment of the king, as you can imagine—and they survived. They didn't even smell like smoke when they came out! And the king acknowledged them and God. A remnant was preserved.

This idea of God having a remnant appears throughout the Bible right up to the last days in which we live, as we will see in the book of Revelation. In short, the remnant is God's chosen faithful people. His true church.

"And the dragon was wroth [really angry] with the woman, and went to make war with the remnant of her seed, which keep the commandments of God, and have the testimony of Jesus Christ" (Revelation 12:17, KJV). Using prophetic imagery, the Bible shows a "remnant" that is fighting against the evil dragon, Satan, who is the enemy of Jesus.

What We Believe

But it makes us ask, what on earth are they a remnant or a leftover from?

As in the examples from the Old Testament, a time is coming when God will need to preserve His people because the world around them will go sour, like drinking grapefruit juice after you've been eating sugary cereal. And this is where we discover what the remnant church is a remnant of. Revelation says, "After this I saw another angel coming down from heaven, having great authority, and the earth was made bright with his glory. And he called out with a mighty voice,

> 'Fallen, fallen is Babylon the great!
> She has become a dwelling place for demons,
> a haunt for every unclean spirit,
> > a haunt for every unclean bird,
> > a haunt for every unclean and detestable beast.'. . .

"Then I heard another voice from heaven saying,

> 'Come out of her, my people,
> lest you take part in her sins, lest you share in her plagues' " (Revelation 18:1, 2, 4).

In prophecy, Babylon represents false religion and sinful ways of living. The Bible tells us that the world will become like the Babylon of old, the ones who captured God's people and tried to make them worship false gods. This is why the angel cries out, "Come out . . . my people!" God's true people will be what are left after people in the world run off to a way of life in opposition to God's. They are the ones left over after everybody else has left Jesus for other things. They have been set apart, called out of the world around them.

> *What do you think makes a religion false? Is it possible to be a Christian and still have false religion? How?*

"Since all these things are thus to be dissolved, what sort of people ought you to be in lives of holiness and godliness, waiting for and hastening the coming of the day of God, because of which the heavens will be set on fire and dissolved, and the heavenly bodies will melt as they burn!" (2 Peter 3:11, 12). To live a life of holiness simply means to live a life set apart for a special purpose and not getting caught up in the sinful messes that this world would love to trap you in. It means living with God's purposes in mind, not just doing whatever you feel like doing. It means following God's way even if everybody else doesn't. That's what God's remnant does.

And you can be sure the devil isn't going to make it easy. The Bible tells us that the devil will start a false religion that mimics Christianity so closely, even the smartest people will fall for it (look at Matthew 24:24). It also says that destructive ways of life will tempt people away from their relationship with God (check 2 Timothy 3:1–5). How will we know where to go and who to listen to? How will people find out about what is going to happen in the last days?

Thankfully, God not only has a special people He has called out, but He has given them a special mission.

Toward the end of the Second World War, the members of the Japanese government began to worry that they would be convicted as war criminals for the way they had mistreated American and British prisoners. They decided to kill the soldiers so they couldn't testify against them. Many soldiers were herded into air raid shelters and burned alive. The U.S. Army realized that if they wanted to save any of the prisoners, they needed to act fast. The camp at Cabanatuan in the Philippines was the closest prison camp, but it was behind enemy lines and was heavily guarded. To make things even more unpleasant, it was in the middle of a flat field—sneaking up on it was almost impossible.

The Japanese knew the Americans were in the area, and so they planned to kill the prisoners before they could be rescued. Rescue seemed impossible, but the American soldiers didn't care and were determined to at least try to save their friends. On January 27, 1945, a small combined American and Philippine group snuck into the jungle toward the enemy army and their captured friends on a special mission.

What We Believe

As the sun set on the horizon, an American plane dropped from the sky and flew low over the Japanese prison camp three times. The Japanese fired their guns into the air and didn't realize that as they were focused on the plane, American soldiers were quickly crawling across the open field. At 7:40 that night, after the sun set, the prisoners inside the camp heard the loudest explosion of gunfire they had ever heard. Within thirty minutes the 511 prisoners were breathing the air of freedom. Four American soldiers, 27 Filipino soldiers, and 1 prisoner were killed in the attack. Almost 530 Japanese soldiers were either killed or wounded. What had seemed impossible had become reality—they had accomplished a special mission that set people free.

God's remnant is like His Special Forces. The Army has Delta Force, but God has Alpha/Omega Force (look at Revelation 1:8); the Navy has the Seals—God has the Sealed (Revelation 7:4)—OK, that's enough. They have a special mission to the world. And it can be summed up in three special messages given by angels in Revelation 14:6–12. In these three messages we find the special mission of the church as well as what identifies it.

The first angel says, " 'Fear God and give him glory, because the hour of his judgment has come, and worship him who made heaven and earth, the sea and the springs of water' " (Revelation 14:7). In other words, the people who follow God won't be bowing down to anyone except the One who gave them a body to bow down with in the first place. The angel also points out that an hour of judgment has come, which tells us that God's people understand that this world is not gonna hang out in outer space forever—an end is approaching.

The second angel repeats what we have already talked about by saying, " 'Fallen, fallen is Babylon the great, she who made all nations drink the wine of the passion of her sexual immorality' " (verse 8). This means God's leftovers understand that they need to be holy—set apart—from the shenanigans that the rest of the world enjoys.

Finally, the third angel reiterates the fallen state of the world, and the punishment for those who persist in following false religions and wicked ways (see verses 9–11). The three messages end with a statement that sums up everything and gives us our final insight into the remnant church. "Here is a call for the endurance of the saints, those who keep the commandments of God and their faith in Jesus" (verse 12). Once again, God's people keep the commandments—from Jesus' commands He gave to His disciples (love God and our neighbors) all the way down to the Ten Commandments (all ten of them).

Jesus tells us in Matthew 28:19 that His followers are to invite anybody in any land to be a part of God's Special Forces, who will carry out His special mission. It certainly won't be easy, as every aspect of being a part of God's remnant goes against the grain of the world. But then again, anything worth doing is seldom easy. And God promises that if we will accept His invitation, He will protect us and bring us into a life of eternal freedom and joy as we help others "come out" of the world and experience those blessings with us.

14 | Unity in the Body of Christ

When I was growing up, my siblings and I played a number of bizarre games unique to my family. While each game had its own set of rules, the common denominator was pain. These games tested the limits of human stupidity in all its shapes, sizes, and forms. One of these little gems was known as Crack the Coconut.

My dad claims it was invented by my grandpa, but no one knows for sure. The idea of the game was for two people to go one on either side of the living room and get on all fours with their head down. Then when the signal was given, the two parties would charge each other like mad bulls in an attempt to bonk heads, thereby "cracking the coconut." The winner was the one who didn't fall over.

No doubt if a parent or teacher is reading this to you or looking over your shoulder, they have either uttered a gasp or said something like "that's just terrible." Then they probably will try to convince you that it never actually happened and this was just some silly game I made up to prove a point that has yet to be mentioned. Actually, I wish I could tell you that I just made this up, but I didn't. We actually played this game. Well, let's say that my brother and stepbrother played this game and I watched.

It was on Christmas when I was about your age that we saw this game come to fruition. While we had known about it, no one had actually worked up the guts to play it. But this year the mood was right. My two siblings tended to get into a good fight every now and then, so when they were in an ornery mood, my dad suggested they work out their frustrations in a friendly game of crack the coconut.

They bought it.

As the elder sibling and the instigator of most trouble, I was elated. It was more exciting than season tickets to your favorite football game. I watched with eager anticipation as they got themselves ready. My grandmother looked on in abject horror and tried to get my dad to end this exercise in insanity. He didn't.

When the signal was given, they launched themselves at each other, and when their two heads struck each other, they made a marvelous *pop!*

No doubt you are concerned about who was the winner of this match, and as I wiped away tears of joy from nearly laughing myself into a coma, my eyes beheld my siblings.

Both had fallen over.

They clutched their heads, and their eyes were rolling around as they groaned in pain. My dad then stepped in and gave a comforting speech that also acted as a lesson.

"Nobody wins!"

I never saw my family play this game or anything like it ever again (even though my brother tried to solicit interest on several occasions). But I have seen God's family play similar games when they are trying to work out their differences.

God's family is made up of people from all over the world. The Bible says, " 'Thus it is written, that the Christ should suffer and on the third day rise from the dead, and that repentance and forgiveness of sins should be proclaimed in his name to all nations, beginning from Jerusalem' " (Luke 24:46, 47). All throughout Scripture there are references to all the nations being included in Christ's forgiveness, thereby welcoming them into the family of God. While this is a beautiful picture that tells us no one is to be excluded, we can't get away from the fact there are differences between individuals.

What We Believe

I have known a few sets of identical twins in my life, and even they have differences in personality, education, and preferences. God's family includes millions of individuals who come from different lands, have different cultures, different tastes, different views, and different ways of communicating, just to name a few. And sometimes these differences don't always complement each other. People get into conflicts over what music to play in church, how the gospel should be preached, and even what to serve at potluck after church. Yet Jesus tells us that we are to be unified as one people.

" 'I will remain in the world no longer, but they are still in the world, and I am coming to you. Holy Father, protect them by the power of your name—the name you gave me—so that they may be one as we are one' " (John 17:11, NIV).

The Bible gives us a clue when it says, "Therefore, if anyone is in Christ, he is a new creation. The old has passed away; behold, the new has come" (2 Corinthians 5:17). While we all have differences from our family histories to our favorite ice creams, we are all new creations in Jesus Christ. While we need to acknowledge our differences, we need to realize that our most important identifying feature is that we are all made in the image of God and made new in our hearts through the Holy Spirit. Not to mention we are all descended from Adam and Eve in the first place, and we are all redeemed through Jesus Christ. Those common factors must outweigh any differences we have. Because that's where the power is.

> *So how can we possibly be one with so many differences?*

When the disciples were walking with Jesus before His crucifixion, they quarreled—a lot. They misunderstood each other and even debated on which one of them was greater than the others. The disciples were made up of loving nurturers and fiery preachers, fishermen and businessmen. The disciples even had a tax collector and a religious zealot following Him. I heard one evangelist say that this combination would be like having George Bush and Saddam Hussein on the same team. And while they had some successes in their time with Jesus, they also had some miserable failures and misunderstandings. But at

Pentecost they finally learned how to act as one—and the result was world changing.

After Jesus ascended to heaven, He told His disciples to wait in Jerusalem for the Holy Spirit. It was a time in their lives that was a little frightening. Christians weren't popular people at that time, and it was very dangerous to follow Christ. Yet Jesus still told them that when the Holy Spirit came they would be Holy witnesses " 'in Jerusalem and in all Judea and Samaria, and to the end of the earth' " (Acts 1:8). This was a *huge* mission, considering there were a relative handful of people who followed Jesus then—roughly 120 people. One hundred twenty people who were supposed to change the world. How could they do this? By uniting together and following Christ's words.

"And when the day of Pentecost was fully come, they were all with one accord in one place" (Acts 2:1, KJV). So what does "one accord" mean? Some translations say it just means they were gathered together in one place. But the Greek word originally used in the book of Acts doesn't mean that. Just because people physically stand around each other doesn't mean there is any unity. There is an old saying, "There can be union without unity: tie two cats together by their tails and throw them over a clothesline." To really accomplish the words of Christ's prayer for oneness, the disciples had to have real unity. The word used in the Pentecost account actually means "to be of one mind." So what does this mean? What does a church that has differences look like when they are of one mind? It has to do with mission.

See, we can have different opinions but one objective; we can have different preferences but the same purpose; and we can have different languages but the same Lord. As a result, these disciples from all walks of life set their differences aside and united in their purpose to wait on God and do His will. The result was that the Holy Spirit was poured out in such a powerful way that thousands came to know Jesus in just one day, and the church began to spread the gospel in a way that would turn the world upside down.

But what do we do with our differences? Do we just set them aside and try to pretend they aren't there? Not at all. We should seek to discover what our differences are and celebrate them and dedicate them to

What We Believe

God so He can use them in a powerful way. "There are different kinds of gifts, but the same Spirit" (1 Corinthians 12:4, NIV). Many of our differences come straight from God Himself to benefit the unity of the body of Christ—the church.

The Bible says that while we all have the same Holy Spirit inside our hearts, we are given unique differences—gifts—that can be used for God's glory. The Bible gives us a great analogy for this when it says, "As it is, there are many parts, yet one body. The eye cannot say to the hand, 'I have no need of you,' nor again the head to the feet, 'I have no need of you.' On the contrary, the parts of the body that seem to be weaker are indispensable, and on those parts of the body that we think less honorable we bestow the greater honor, and our unpresentable parts are treated with greater modesty, which our more presentable parts do not require. But God has so composed the body, giving greater honor to the part that lacked it, that there may be no division in the body, but that the members may have the same care for one another. If one member suffers, all suffer together; if one member is honored, all rejoice together" (1 Corinthians 12:20–26).

> *How do you think your church would be different if it united like the disciples? What would it look like?*

Every part of our bodies is interconnected in an amazing way. Consider when someone dies of heart failure. Their fingers and arms and legs were just fine, yet that one part failing caused the whole body to fail. The same thing would happen if your lungs, arteries, or brain stopped as well. And even if you just lost a limb, an eye, or a hand, it would affect the way you function as a whole.

God's church is made up of several individual parts that are called to work together—within their unique differences—to accomplish the same purpose. It is an unstoppable and beautiful force when it happens, and it gives God glory. I hope that as you learn more about where God has called and gifted you to be in the church, you will let the Holy Spirit use your differences for the unity and purpose of the church and not get stuck butting heads with your brothers and sisters in Jesus. Because when that happens, nobody wins.

15 | Baptism

A pastor friend of mine once told me about a time he baptized a very large woman and had a little trouble. Everything was going normally at first. The pastor shared a few inspirational words and then invited the lady being baptized into the tank of water. He gently led her to his side, said a few more words and then, using his hand to support her back, eased her backwards under the water. But there was one little snag—literally. The woman's baptismal robe caught on a nail sticking out of the wall, which resulted in an amusing scene for the congregation.

First, the force of the snag on her robe caused her feet to slip in the baptismal tank. This meant that instead of gliding easily into the water, she flew backwards with her feet flying up in the air. The pastor, who couldn't support the momentum of her weight, was nearly dragged under because his arm was underneath her. The only thing that saved both of them from drowning—or an even more embarrassing experience—was that the other, more experienced pastor reached out and pulled my pastor friend back to his feet. As you can imagine, the lady being baptized came up sputtering and coughing while the ministers did their best to smile and pretend like nothing out of the ordinary had happened. Before she could protest, the pastors gave her hugs and a hearty "amen" and sent her out of the tank. Then the pastor said the only thing he could say.

"Who's next?"

Needless to say there were probably a few souls that day who were reluctant to follow this woman's example and get into the tank.

Some of the first words Jesus spoke to His followers were, "Follow Me." They are interesting words to be sure, because you can't be totally sure of what you're in for. As a follower you have to agree to go wherever your leader goes and do whatever he does. But Jesus' disciples knew from the moment they met Jesus that He was someone worth following.

They followed Jesus no matter the cost. They left family, they cast out demons, and some were exiled or even killed as a result of following Jesus. They even obeyed Him when it didn't make sense—such as bringing Him a sack lunch when there were thousands of people to be fed; or casting fishing nets on one side of the fishing boat when the other side hadn't yielded any fish all night. But one of the most important things they followed Jesus in was baptism.

The Bible says, "Then Jesus came from Galilee to the Jordan to John, to be baptized by him" (Matthew 3:13). Jesus was dunked under water at the beginning of His ministry on earth, and the experience was so meaningful and important to Him that He told His disciples, " 'Go therefore and make disciples of all nations, baptizing them in the name of the Father and of the Son and of the Holy Spirit, teaching them to observe all that I have commanded you. And behold, I am with you always, to the end of the age' " (Matthew 28:19, 20). And His followers did.

When Peter preached his powerful Pentecost sermon (when the Holy Spirit gave power to the disciples), he told those listening, " 'Repent and *be baptized* every one of you in the name of Jesus Christ for the forgiveness of your sins, and you will receive the gift of the Holy Spirit' " (Acts 2:38; emphasis added). Peter links accepting Jesus with being baptized.

Baptism

The apostle Paul, giving a defense of his faith to the Greek people said, " ' "And now why do you wait? Rise and be baptized and wash away your sins, calling on his name" ' " (Acts 22:16). Paul encouraged his listeners not to delay at all, but rather get into the water and be baptized as they heard his gospel presentation.

Now this seems cut and dried. To follow Jesus, we must follow His example, His Word, and the words of His disciples, and that means being baptized. But, in my experience, I have run into a lot of people who are either terrified of being baptized or simply have the wrong idea about what baptism will do for them. This is why, before we explore what baptism is, we have to look at what baptism is not.

First we must understand that baptism is *not* magic water. I once had a gentleman whom I had never seen before show up at my office determined to get baptized. "I *need* to get baptized, Pastor. I just need to." I asked him why it was so important to him. He didn't answer me except to repeat, "I just *need* to get baptized." The man had some troubles in his life, and so I took this as an opportunity to explain that while baptism is an important step in following Jesus, it doesn't give you any special powers or special abilities. He looked thoughtful for a moment, said, "OK," and left, never to return. It was an interesting encounter to say the least. It made me wonder what he thought baptism actually did.

> *What do you think scares people about baptism?*

The water in the baptismal tank isn't magic. Jesus was baptized in the Jordan River, a very muddy, dirty river. And most baptismal tanks I've seen, even if they've been cleaned, still have bits of lint and fuzz floating around in them when they are full of water. The water is just water—nothing more. Well, usually it's heated in a baptismal tank—so I guess that's special.

The second thing baptism is not: a status symbol saying, "I have arrived."

Once, three pastors in the South were having lunch in a diner. One said, "Ya know, since summer started I've been having trouble with bats

What We Believe

in my loft and attic at church. I've tried everything—noise, spray, cats—nothing seems to scare them away."

Another said, "Yeah, me too. I've got hundreds living in my belfry and in the narthex attic. I've even had the place fumigated, and they won't go away."

The third said, "I baptized all mine and made them members of the church. Haven't seen one back since." This might seem like a strange joke to you, but there is a lot of truth in it. Many times when people get baptized they think it means that they are done growing in Jesus. They have "arrived." As a result, they never come back to church and no one hears from them again. They think they've completed some sort of program. The truth is, no one will ever arrive until we are in heaven talking with Jesus face to face—and even then we will have a lot to learn.

What can we do to continue to grow in our faith after baptism?

Finally, we come to the most important thing baptism is not. This is what makes so many people scared to get baptized. It is the idea that when you get baptized, you must never make another mistake. I don't know how many kids and even adults I have talked to who feel they can't get baptized because they are not perfect. It is a horrible lie the devil has used to make sincere people afraid of making a full commitment to Jesus. The very idea of getting baptized has to do with you admitting that you need Jesus to save you from sin and to be Lord of your life. It is *not* a symbol of perfection. Which brings us to what baptism is.

"Do you not know that all of us who have been baptized into Christ Jesus were baptized into his death? We were buried therefore with him by baptism into death, in order that, just as Christ was raised from the dead by the glory of the Father, we too might walk in newness of life. For if we have been united with him in a death like his, we shall certainly be united with him in a resurrection like his" (Romans 6:3–5).

The Bible lets us know that baptism is a symbol of the death and resurrection of Jesus Christ; and it is a crucial part of following Him.

Baptism

It's not important just because Jesus told us to do it—and to deny it would be refusing to follow Him—but it is important because it is the public symbol that you have made a decision to follow Jesus no matter what the cost.

When you are put under the water (the word *baptized* means to be submerged), it is symbolic of you dying to sin. It's a statement saying, "I want to live the type of life Jesus lived." Then when you are brought back out of the water, it symbolizes a commitment to live a life that looks like Christ's. There is a difference between being committed to living like Christ and perfectly living the life of Christ. Being committed means that you know you will have temptations and mess-ups, but you are willing to ask Jesus for forgiveness and to try again. Perfectly living like Christ means you are . . . well . . . perfect. I have yet to see anyone, including the disciples and apostles in the Bible, live a mistake-free life after baptism. You will still need grace and forgiveness after baptism. Baptism does not mean you no longer need a Savior; rather, it is recognizing that you have one.

Being baptized is also a public declaration of your faith. It is a statement to the world that says you belong to Jesus and are one of His disciples. And when people see you being baptized and making a commitment to follow Jesus, they will be inspired to do the same. What's so scary about that?

I was baptized May 11, 1991—the same month and day as my dad. And when I did, I didn't feel pressured in any way. I had been studying the Bible, and I understood that if I wanted to grow in Christ and truly be one of His disciples, I would have to partake in the symbol of baptism. For me it made about as much sense as getting your driver's license when you turn sixteen. It was a part of growing up spiritually, and I wanted to do it.

Afterwards my family had a nice meal and we celebrated, because baptism represented my official decision to be a part of God's family and one of His followers. Now, as the years went by I experienced temptation and sin, and I even stopped attending church for a while. The good news is that God doesn't just let His family members go. He worked on me through all sorts of special circumstances; and now I'm

What We Believe

a pastor and I get to baptize kids who are just as excited about Christ as I was when I was eleven.

I also know these kids will face struggles and might even leave off their relationship with Jesus. But the cool thing is that just as you make a commitment to follow Jesus through baptism, He has made a commitment to you as your Lord and Savior; and He will be with you wherever you go, guiding you back to Him.

I hope you will make the decision to be baptized. I hope you will make a decision to follow Jesus and not be afraid to grow in your relationship with Him. I have never regretted it. And while it didn't give me superpowers, it has a special place in my heart and truly was a life-changing experience. God has been very good to me; and I have no doubt that if you are willing to follow Him, you will see just how good He is, too.

16 | The Lord's Supper

Are you familiar with the "kids' table"? It's an unstable device that adults break out on major holidays such as Thanksgiving, Christmas, Easter, and occasionally at lunch after church. It is a tool designed to segregate the civilized from the silly, the sophisticated from the savage—the adult from the ankle biter and adolescent. And I think you've probably sat at one before.

In my circle of family and friends it always took the form of a card table with retractable legs. It was set up adjacent to the beautiful dining room table, which was perfectly acceptable for my siblings to eat at any day of the year besides holidays. On those holidays, while the adult table was laden with fine china and fancy glass goblets, our little runt of a surface was adorned with an assortment of plates and dinnerware made from paper and plastic. To top things off, instead of sparkling goblets, we got shiny plastic cups. Special.

As dinner began and all the adults sat down to their well-stocked table (which was also where all the food was being held captive) we kids sat down to enjoy the meal on our plates, which we did. What we did not enjoy was the wobbling. That little table tried the best it could, but heaven help you if your foot brushed against one of the four skinny legs because it would send an earthquake rumbling throughout the entire structure. If you weren't quick to grab your plastic cup it would spill everywhere, only proving to the adults that you were not ready for their table. It was all a setup, a test to see if we were worthy. One must master the cup of juice and plate of food—even in a crisis situation—if one is to sit at the adult table. Remember that proverb.

Eventually the day came (I think I was in college) when I was moved to the adult table, and only then because there weren't enough adults to go around that year. I was beaming with pride as I clutched my glass goblet with such intensity that it nearly fused to my hand—but at least it didn't spill. And I regaled my adult table-sitters with intelligent conversation. No talk of bodily functions this year (which is a staple of conversation at the kids' table). Nope, it was all current events, history, and the latest in film as I sipped my sparkling grape juice and actually ate with silverware instead of my hands. I was just so happy to be included at this special table that symbolized the transition and partaking of adulthood, of another phase of life . . . at least until more adults showed up and demoted me.

An important event occurs in churches that involves a special meal. We call it the Lord's Supper, and it is taken right out of the Gospels. Jesus was having His last meal with His closest friends, the disciples. They were all "reclined at the table" (Luke 22:14, NIV), the Lord's table, that He had reserved for His friends (look up Luke 22:10–12), when Jesus stood up and made a few observations about the meal that He would like His friends to, well, observe.

First He grabbed the bread they were munching on, blessed it, and divided it up. He says, "Take, eat: this is my body" (Mark 14:22, KJV). As if that wasn't strange enough, He then does something with the drink.

Holding His goblet full of grape juice in the air, He makes one of the strangest toasts ever recorded. "And he took a cup, and when he had given thanks he gave it to them, and they all drank of it. And he said to them, 'This is my blood of the covenant, which is poured out for many' "

The Lord's Supper

(Mark 14:23, 24). Normally a toast like that would get you sent back to the kids' table for being gross. But Jesus was alluding to something beautiful.

Although His disciples didn't totally understand it, Jesus was going to die—in a cruel way. His blood was going to be spilled and His body was going to be broken for us. Jesus was going to die on our behalf, and the cup symbolized that. By drinking it His disciples were saying, "I accept and partake of Your sacrifice on the cross on my behalf." It was a serious thought, even sad—and yet, what an offer. Jesus asked them to sit at His table and eat the food that symbolized the accepting of His death on the cross for mankind. That's an even better deal than the adult table. But why the symbols? Why not just tell them straight and leave it at that?

Jesus said, " 'Do this in remembrance of me' " (Luke 22:19). Humans forget things. God knows that we do—He made us and works with us every day in a million ways. We forget everything from the answers on tests at school (which we forgot to study for) all the way down to forgetting each other's names. So, Jesus instituted the Lord's Supper as a way to remind us of His sacrifice, as well as His open invitation to partake of it. God's table is not exclusive to perfect people, just to those who want to accept Him as their Lord.

And the meal doesn't end there. Traditionally at my house after a big meal, everyone finds a patch of carpet or a corner of couch to sprawl out on. Then we groan and moan for a while as we all come to the realization that once again we have eaten an obscene amount of food. After the Lord's Supper, Jesus skipped the sprawling-out stage and enacted what we call the ordinance of humility, which is just a fancy phrase that means good old-fashioned footwashing.

"Then he poured water into a basin and began to wash the disciples' feet and to wipe them with the towel that was wrapped around him. . . . Peter said to him, 'You shall never wash my feet.' Jesus answered him, 'If I do not wash you, you have no share with me.' Simon Peter said to him, 'Lord, not my feet only but also my hands and my head!' . . . 'If I then, your Lord and Teacher, have washed your feet, you also ought to wash one another's feet' " (John 13:5, 8, 9, 14).

What We Believe

Feet are generally gross. Human feet contain approximately two hundred and fifty thousand sweat glands that excrete as much as half a pint of moisture every day. Mmm, I can smell 'em already. One in four people suffer from foot fungus (known as athlete's foot) at some point in their life. Bet that's nice to look at. And then there is the wide variety of abnormal toe shapes, sizes, and numbers. In Bible times people wore sandals everywhere they went in the dust and the dirt, and they didn't have antibacterial medications. Jesus sat down and washed *those* gross things and, according to the Bible, asked His disciples to do the same—which is why this makes for a powerful symbol.

Sin is gross, and we have it all over us. But Jesus cleanses us through His sacrificial blood, and He serves us as our Lord and Friend. He asks His disciples to continue the practice as a reminder of their sins being cleansed as well as reminding them how important it is to serve each other in love as He demonstrated. Since God's disciples are still around today—you and me—we are called to partake of these symbols every now and then as a time of reflection for what Jesus has done for us.

It is a special occasion when it happens—the most important dinner appointment you can make, even though we only eat a little bit during the special service. And it's important to prepare for important occasions.

When I worked at camp we had line call every morning at seven thirty, and the staff was expected to be dressed appropriately in our staff shirts. One morning my friend Joe trudged down the hill in what he felt was an outfit that expressed himself better than the blue staff polos we had to wear. He had on Mr. Clean pajama bottoms, a tie, and no shirt whatsoever. It was priceless and hilarious—to the staff anyway. Our camp director wasn't as thrilled and ran out to meet him and told him to go put on some more "appropriate" attire. And I suppose he had a point.

So what do we wear to the Lord's Supper? It's not so much what's on your body as what's in your heart. Since the service has to do with forgiveness and service to others, it might be good to check and see if you

The Lord's Supper

have been holding on to something in your life that you know is wrong and ask God for forgiveness. Or maybe you are at odds with a sibling or a friend, in which case you might want to talk things out with them and make it right before coming to the Lord's table. Whatever the case may be, the good news is that, unlike the adult table at my parents' house, the Lord's table is open to any follower of God from any background. Young and old, male and female, rich and poor, beautiful and the less than beautiful are all not only welcome but also desired at Jesus' special supper. I know because He told His disciples that. "And he said to them, 'I have earnestly desired to eat this Passover with you before I suffer' " (Luke 22:15).

> *How can we make the Lord's Supper a celebration while still keeping it a time of meaningful meditation?*

Jesus still passionately desires for His disciples—you and me—to come and sit at His table and partake of His special supper.

17 | Spiritual Gifts and Ministries

Have you ever participated in a white elephant gift exchange? You know, where people buy the worst and cheapest gifts imaginable and then exchange them at parties and holidays? It's a sick tradition in my family to do this on Christmas. Every year someone is the lucky recipient of a little can labeled "meat product." What is it? Nobody knows. Nobody wants to find out. So, year after year it is repackaged and shamelessly given to someone else. But it's not just my family who practice this warped gift giving.

My wife and I have two good friends named Mikey and Daniela. One year for Daniela's birthday, I went to Goodwill and bought a glass bear that used to be full of Avon perfume but now just sat there empty and useless. An Avon bear. It was the *perfect* gift.

To say she was confused when she opened the package and pulled out this random bear would be an understatement. I videotaped her reaction to the gift, and it was a combination of confusion and contempt. She was especially surprised when her friend grabbed it and pulled the bear's head off to reveal the cap where you could refill the bear with perfume—or soda, as I suggested. She didn't think either of those ideas was acceptable. She really didn't think any suggestion we had was acceptable, and so the bear sat there—useless—and waited until my birthday, when she repacked it and gave it to me.

As of a couple weeks ago, the bear has found its way into Mikey and Daniela's new home as a house-warming present. I suspect the dumb bear might find its way back to me in the near future. This exchange of a useless gift could go on forever, for all I know.

To be honest, it is kinda of fun. It certainly makes gift giving a lot easier for whoever has the bear. When it comes to giving gifts, it is always much easier to give a silly or bad gift to someone. It is the special, personal, and meaningful gifts that are hard to come by.

Around the time I was thinking about proposing to my wife, we had a talk about the sort of engagement gift she would like. Getting engaged is a *huge* milestone, and it had to be marked with something thoughtful, sweet, and meaningful. She decided that instead of a ring or a watch, she wanted an antique locket she could put our pictures in.

"No problem," I said ignorantly, thinking that this task would pose no problem for a treasure hunter such as I. "I'm sure I will be able to find something special when the time is right."

About three months into my search for this ridiculous locket I was starting to think that the right time would never come. I had tried store after store, antique shop after antique shop, and had no luck. See, I knew Angela's taste, I knew what she was thinking, and I knew how much I loved her, and all those factors meant that no ordinary locket would do—it had to be special and unique. This was hard to do, since just about every nice locket I found looked the same as all the others.

For a while I thought about just giving up and getting her a nice card with some money it. It wouldn't be romantic in the slightest, but at least I wouldn't have the stress of finding the perfect gift. Thankfully, as I was filling out the card I stumbled upon eBay and found a beautiful silver antique locket from the 1800s. After a few clicks of the mouse, the locket was sent to me, and I had great success as I presented it to my bride-to-be.

What We Believe

Despite the difficulties, it is possible to give the "perfect gift." I'm sure people have given you some strange things in your life, but I bet also that you have been given some very nice things that mean a lot to you. You've probably given things to others that have been meaningful to them. You have been given education, clothes, and the chance to study the Bible to know more about Jesus. These are all gifts that keep on giving because you use them again and again.

The Bible says that God is the Master Gift-Giver. " 'If you then, who are evil, know how to give good gifts to your children, how much more will the heavenly Father give the Holy Spirit to those who ask him!' " (Luke 11:13). This means that if we human beings, with all our problems, know the difference between giving a good gift and a bad gift, how much more does the God who created us know how to give gifts. The text even tells us what one of His greatest gifts is—the Holy Spirit.

Now we already talked about the Holy Spirit in chapter 5—how He works to make us like Jesus, guides our lives, and empowers us to share God's love. But one of the greatest things about the Holy Spirit is that while He is a gift from God the Father who does all those amazing things—He in turn gives us gifts Himself!

"Now there are varieties of gifts, but the same Spirit; and there are varieties of service, but the same Lord; and there are varieties of activities, but it is the same God who empowers them all in everyone. To each is given the manifestation of the Spirit for the common good" (1 Corinthians 12:4–7). Talk about a gift that keeps on giving!

The Holy Spirit has a gift list that not even Santa Claus could deliver. According to the Bible, the Holy Spirit has such gifts as prophecy, wisdom, teaching, love, and the working of miracles, just to name a few. And even within those gifts are unique gifts. For example, if you have the gift of wisdom, you might have the gift of sharing it through writing, speaking, or any number of different media. Or if you have the gift of love, you might also have the gift of expressing it through acts of kindness, encouraging words to people who are discouraged, or even sacrificing your life for them—the possibilities are endless!

Spiritual Gifts and Ministries

A good way to look at these gifts is as talents and abilities that God gives you through His Spirit to help share the message of Jesus Christ. And the beautiful thing is that each person has their unique, meaningful, and personalized version of the gifts listed in the Bible: "And there are varieties of activities, but it is the same God who empowers them all in everyone" (1 Corinthians 12:6). Did you catch that? There are varieties of activities, and *everyone* is empowered. So how do we discover what they are? A lot of people aren't aware that God has granted them special abilities to use for Him.

> *What could you do to let people know they have been given special abilities by God?*

The first thing to do in discovering your spiritual gift is simply to pray and ask God to fill you with the Holy Spirit. Then, ask God to help you discover the special abilities He has placed in you. You might want to ask your parents, friends, or teachers what they think—see if a pattern emerges. Another cool tool out there is called a spiritual gifts inventory, which is something every Christian needs to take. It asks you certain questions and helps you narrow down the area in which you are gifted. When you do discover it, then the Holy Spirit will show you how to use it. It's extremely important to use your gifts.

Jesus tells a story in Matthew 25 about a guy who entrusted three men with his money—called talents in the Bible—while he went away. The first guy had five talents and went and invested it and doubled what he had. The second guy, who had two talents, invested his money also, and he too doubled his money. Things are looking pretty good for the man who trusted these men . . . until we come to guy number three. This little stinker dug a hole in the ground and threw his one little talent in the ground and buried it.

When the man came back, he was excited to find out what the first and second man had done with his money. He praised their efforts and celebrated with them. But when he came to the third guy, he was not pleased. The third guy went and dug up his measly little coin and tried to make an excuse, saying, "I know you are a shrewd businessman, so I didn't want to risk any of your money—so I hid it." Can you guess what the man did? What would you have done?

Well, the third guy was fired as a financial manager right then and there. Then the man took the measly little coin and gave it to the one who had doubled his to ten. Then Jesus said, " 'For to everyone who has will more be given, and he will have an abundance. But from the one who has not, even what he has will be taken away' " (Matthew 25:29). Essentially this means that when you don't use it—you lose it. And it can be applied to our abilities we get from God.

God wants so badly for us to share His love, so He equips us with gifts to get it done. But, when someone stalls or isn't using what they have, God takes it away and gives it to someone who will use it. Make sense?

The gifts we are given are like spiritual muscles—the more we use them, the stronger they get. The best preachers in the world didn't start as great speakers, but as they practiced and developed their gifts they grew more and more powerful. The same goes for writers, painters, athletes, and anybody else who is successful. As we exercise our spiritual gifts, they will be become stronger, have more influence, and take us and the church places we can't imagine. And it's important to be strong, because the church needs all the help you and I can give it through our gifts.

The apostle Paul said, "So with yourselves, since you are eager for manifestations of the Spirit, try to excel in building up the church" (1 Corinthians 14:12). Why is it important to build up the church with our spiritual muscles? Because the devil doesn't want God's church delivering His message of love. He tries to attack it with discouragement, false ideas, and distorted pictures of God.

I remember when my younger brother was having trouble getting one of his friends to leave our apartment. His friend was probably ten and refused to leave. He was teasing my brother and being obstinate. This troublemaking kid laughed with glee and threatened that he was going to stay until he felt like leaving. Since my mom was at work, my brother was having difficulty acquiring help to get this intruder out. He didn't have the muscle to get this boy out of our home. But I did.

Spiritual Gifts and Ministries

I remember getting the call for help. I had been secretly listening to the exchange in the hall, and so I knew the situation already. I calmly walked out to the entryway where the little brat was standing defiantly. His arms were crossed, and he had an arrogant smirk on his face. I wasn't impressed. See, I was fourteen and outweighed this kid by a good thirty or forty pounds. So, without saying a word, I opened the door out into the hallway. I grabbed the kid by his shirt, lifting his feet off the ground, and flung him out into the outside hallway so hard he hit the wall, dazed and confused. Then I shut the door and locked it. Problem solved.

The devil would like to get a foothold into the door of God's church—God's family. But when we strive to develop our spiritual gifts we develop spiritual power. We get better at working together and deepening our understanding of God's will for our lives and the life of the church. So when the enemy comes, trying to get into God's family, he is met with a bunch of people who, *through the Holy Spirit*, have enough wisdom to recognize him and his lies, and enough power and courage to throw him out on his rear end.

So what's your spiritual gift? Do you have any idea? Take time as soon as you can to pray and ask God for the Holy Spirit to come into your life and reveal the special ability God wants you to have. I know He has one picked out especially for you. Then, dedicate that gift to God to use in the building up of His church and the spreading of His message of love to the world. I guarantee He will open doors for you to use it in your church, in your family, and in your interactions with everybody you meet.

God is a Master Gift-Giver. And I know the gift He has designed especially for you will be used for great things. When you see Him working through it, you won't want to exchange it for anything. Not even an Avon bear.

18 | The Gift of Prophecy

In September 2006 Elizabeth Shoaf was accosted on her way home from school by a man dressed as a police officer. He told her that he would escort her home. But they would be going a scenic route—a very scenic route.

This strange man took Elizabeth deep into the woods, where he revealed that he was not in fact a cop. Rather, he was a kidnapping lunatic who was wanted by the law. He revealed this to Elizabeth not by telling her so much as by shoving her into a fifteen-foot-deep pit in the side of a hill that was covered with plywood. The bunker had a hand-dug privy with toilet paper, a camp stove, and shelves made with cut branches and canvas. Then the man—a Mr. Vinson Filyaw—covered it up so no one could see them.

Poor Elizabeth spent ten days in that miserable place, wondering if she would ever see her loved ones again. Adding to the fear was her gruesome host, whose previous crimes involved criminal sexual misconduct. The authorities had tried to arrest him before, but he had escaped through a tunnel in his bedroom that led out to his shed. All seemed hopeless for this poor teenager being held by a crazed tunnel-

The Gift of Prophecy

digging criminal ... until one evening, when she made a bold move.

Somehow, when Vinson was asleep, Elizabeth procured an item of his that made her the most dangerous person in the world.

A teenage girl with a cell phone.

Swift as could be, she cranked out the most important message of her life, a text message to her mother explaining where she was and what was going on. Shortly after, Vinson awoke and discovered her holding his telecommunication device. All would have been lost if Vinson was an intelligent human being; thankfully he wasn't as good at common sense as he was at tunnel digging.

"I'm just playing a game," Elizabeth said, which was partially true. She was playing Bust a Criminal, which is always a fun game to play. Vinson bought this story and went back about his business. It didn't take long for the authorities to show up and do a little communicating of their own—with handcuffs and jail time. You can imagine the tears and relief experienced by Elizabeth and her family, and how grateful they all were that Elizabeth had a way to communicate the most important message of her life to them.

Now besides helping you build an airtight case for your parents to buy you a cell phone, this story demonstrates how important it is to receive messages from those we care about and those who care about us. We have devised numerous ways to prevent our missing the messages that have an impact on our lives. In addition to text messaging, we have answering machines, pagers, voice mail, memo pads, and Post-it notes.

God is in the message business as well. He gave us His Word, and He gave us His Son to communicate His love for us. He sends us His Spirit so we can receive the message properly. But one of the most incredible ways He communicates with us is through His prophets.

The Bible says, "Long ago, at many times and in many ways, God spoke to our fathers by the prophets" (Hebrews 1:1). But it wasn't just in the good ol' days that God used prophets to speak to us. Concerning God's church at the end of time, Revelation says, "Then the dragon became furious with the woman and went off to make war with the rest of her offspring, on those who keep the commandments of God and hold to the testimony of Jesus" (Revelation 12:17). We interpret the dragon as being the devil, and the woman as the church. One of the reasons that nasty dragon is after God's people is that they hold to the "testimony of Jesus."

So what *is* the testimony of Jesus? Thankfully God never gives us incomplete messages, and He lets us know what it is in Revelation 19:10: "For the testimony of Jesus is the spirit of prophecy." The Spirit of prophecy is a part of God's last-day church.

One of my biggest frustrations when I'm trying to figure out the meaning of a word happens when I go to the dictionary and in the definition of the word I'm trying to define is *another* word that makes even less sense than the one I originally looked up. I'm afraid that we are on a similar journey because now that we've established what the testimony of Jesus is, we need to figure out what the Spirit of prophecy is.

First off, note that the Spirit of prophecy is just that—a spirit. It isn't a human being or animal, vegetable, or mineral. Second, the only place we will get a good definition for a holy term is in the Holy Bible.

"Now there are varieties of gifts, but the same Spirit; . . . To each is given the manifestation of the Spirit for the common good. To one is given through the Spirit the utterance of wisdom, . . . to another the working of miracles, to another prophecy" (1 Corinthians 12:4, 7, 8, 10). Essentially this is a review of the gifts the Holy Spirit gives each one of us; and among them is mentioned prophecy. In a nutshell, the Spirit of prophecy is *the gift of prophecy given by the Holy Spirit.*

I have received a lot of "special" gifts in my life. One of my ongoing battles occurs with my family around Christmas. I am often asked for something that no doubt many of you are asked for—a list. It's a piece of paper chronicling your heart's desires that you hope end up under the tree. I'm not sure where the communication breakdown occurs, but every year I am greeted by gifts under the tree that were not on my list. Not only were they not on my list, but they weren't on anyone's list. I have no idea where they came from or what possessed my well-meaning

The Gift of Prophecy

relatives to procure such an item. I have received everything from hand-knitted sweaters in blinding colors that could get you a beating if you wore it to school to books by authors no one has heard of—for good reason. It's not that I'm ungrateful; I just don't understand the gifts I get sometimes. Likewise, the gift of prophecy tends to be a spiritual gift people have trouble with.

The person who possesses the gift of prophecy, known as a prophet, has a complex job that can be easily misunderstood, since it's not a typical career choice among high school and college grads. You seldom find accredited four-year degrees in prophetic administration.

Once again the Bible offers some insight into the career of the prophets. They receive visions of the future and messages and warnings for the present; they represent and speak for God, encourage the church and God's followers, and in general help people to do what God wants them to do. A good way to sum it up is by calling them "God's special messenger."

God gave such a messenger early in our church's development, and her name is Ellen White. She was born in 1827 and died in 1915. During her lifetime she had approximately two thousand visions from God. In addition to these insights from God via His Spirit, she wrote five thousand articles, forty books, and more than fifty thousand pages of other material on topics ranging from evangelism to eggs. What makes this even more amazing is that due to a childhood injury, she only completed third grade. I know some brilliant people who have Ph.D.'s and have only managed to write thirty books in their lifetime. She helped to shape and form the Seventh-day Adventist Church through her gift and has touched the lives of millions. But, besides these amazing statistics, are there any proofs that she was a prophet?

When I was pastoring a church early in my career, a man came into the church office claiming to be a prophet. His claim was far more interesting than anything the staff was working on at the time, so we agreed to meet with him. One of his messages to us was that after study and hearing from the Lord, he now knew the exact identity of the antichrist—the evil person who will impersonate Jesus Christ in the very last days of this world's history. The truth about the antichrist is a very

What We Believe

important truth indeed, so we all leaned forward to hear this divine revelation. So what was the identity of the antichrist?

Michael Jackson.

Now, I'll give the man this much: I find Michael Jackson to be rather disturbing, and he has a face that would scare the Grim Reaper. But I cannot, through Scripture, establish the King of Pop as the antichrist.

This is one of the key tests of a prophet: "To the teaching and to the testimony! If they will not speak according to this word, it is because they have no dawn" (Isaiah 8:20). A biblical prophet says things in harmony with God's Word. Ellen White described her own ministry as a "lesser light to lead men and women to the greater light."* Her writings do not replace the Bible, but they are in harmony with it.

Another test for a prophet is to see what direction their ministry points to. Have you ever been given the wrong directions? Maybe it was in a recipe—they either had you put in the wrong ingredient or they left the right ingredient out. Or perhaps it had to do with swimming lessons. Instead of telling you to blow out of your nose when you dove into the pool, your instructor told you to breathe in, which resulted in a fear of water that haunts you to this day. Whatever the case may be, we have all received bad directions. But the worst direction of all is the one that does not point to Christ.

The Bible says, "So whether you eat or drink or whatever you do, do it all for the glory of God" (1 Corinthians 10:31, NIV). Our talents are given to us to always use for God's glory. A person can have many unattractive traits—a big nose, a big gut, a big toe—but the worst is a big head. So does Ellen White demonstrate a humble attitude that gives Christ glory? Let's look at a sample of her messages.

"Only the covering which Christ Himself has provided can make us meet to appear in God's presence. This covering, the robe of His own righteousness, Christ will put upon every repenting, believing soul. . . . This robe, woven in the loom of heaven, has in it not one thread of human devising."†

---

* *The Review and Herald,* Jan. 20, 1903.
† Quoted in *Maranatha,* p. 78.

The Gift of Prophecy

Ellen White gave absolute credit to Jesus for salvation. And when it came to her view on herself, she was very humble.

"In regard to infallibility, I never claimed it; God alone is infallible. His word is true, and in him is no variableness, or shadow of turning."*

Ellen White was a balanced woman, who knew where her special gift came from. And even though she wrote so much and inspired so many, some people struggle with accepting her gift. I don't know many people who dislike chocolate, ice cream, pizza, the beach, or video games, but some do. It's downright sick to think about the joy these people are missing. When it comes to a unique gift given by God, we should be aware that not everyone appreciates it, for a variety of reasons. I have found there are usually two objections—and they both have to do with misunderstandings.

> *Can you think of any other traits a prophet might or should have?*

The first is context. Whenever we read any of Ellen White's comments—or the Bible for that matter—it is good to ask a couple of questions, like, "Who were they writing to?" and "What was the situation?" The reason to ask is that many of Ellen White's messages were given more than a hundred years ago. While this doesn't change the importance and relevance of her messages for us today, it does affect how we understand them. For example, in one letter she wrote, "You would not be purchasing bicycles, which you could do without, but would be receiving the blessing of God in exercising your physical powers in a less expensive way."† Did Mrs. White have a deep and abiding hatred for the two-wheeled contraption that most of us own? Not at all. What problem was she addressing? Back then a bike was a fairly new invention and cost so much money that people were going broke and into debt to buy them. The issue was the right use of their money—they didn't have good ol' Wal-Mart back then. Today she might actually tell you to go buy a bike versus buying some of the expensive cars people

---

* *1888 Materials*, letter to F. E. Beldon.
† *The Review and Herald*, Aug. 21, 1894.

dump money into today. If you understand the *context* of her comment, you know that Ellen White was not against bicycles but against a poor use of money.

Another context issue that befuddles people happens both with the Bible and with Ellen White's messages. Did you know that you can make the Bible say anything you want? It's true. If I take a few words from Genesis 4:25 and add part of Proverbs 31:10, I can create a sentence that says: "A son . . . called . . . Seth . . . is far more precious than jewels."

Now while I may be more precious than jewels, the Bible clearly is *not* saying that. Genesis 4:25 refers to Adam's son Seth, and Proverbs 31:10 is talking about a good wife—something I can never be no matter how hard I try. But by pulling these phrases out of context I have created a false truth. People often do this with Ellen White's words—taking her statements from here and there and assembling ideas that she never promoted.

Recently I saw a book like this, self-published by the author, about angels. Most of the sentences were actually composed of several sentences from Ellen White's writings. I was stunned. An example might be, "Angels . . . are coming . . . to get . . . you." This would actually be composed from four different statements taken out of their proper context. People have tried to build a case against Mrs. White based on false arguments like these. It isn't fair, and it isn't true. The Ellen G. White Estate Web site (http://www.whiteestate.org/) deals with these issues and more, if you would like an interesting study on this topic. Just click "Issues & Answers" on the homepage.

The second issue is how we use Ellen White's words. Some people believe her writings should be included in the Bible, and they sometimes place her messages above the Bible. Others don't think her ideas should be used at all. So what is the best way to study the words from God's special messenger? The prophet's own words tell us best. "The Lord desires you to study your Bibles. He has not given any additional light to take the place of His Word. This light [Ellen White's writing] is to bring confused minds to His Word, which, if eaten and digested, is as the lifeblood of the soul. Then good works will be seen as light shining in darkness."* In other words, her writings simply help us understand what is already in the Bible, and in our study the Bible is first and foremost. If we should get confused about something the Bible says, Ellen White's messages can help us understand.

God sends us special messages every day through our friends and family; through music and nature; and through His Word and His messenger. Our enemy the devil does everything he can to prevent us from receiving God's beautiful words by casting doubt in our hearts and trying to distort the message. But if we humbly approach God's messages with an open heart and an open mind, aware that our enemy is trying to confuse us, we will receive the message and be set free from any trap the enemy may set, just as Elizabeth was set free from hers.

---

*Selected Messages, book 3, 1980, p. 29.

19 | The Law of God

Did you know that it is illegal to get a fish drunk in Ohio? Or that in Florida, men may not be seen publicly in any kind of strapless gown? From not being able to slurp your soup in New Jersey to not being allowed to take a picture of a rabbit between January and April in Wyoming—all of these laws were created to somehow benefit people. Trouble is, we really don't know the reason anymore.

These bizarre laws were created a long time ago, and today they make about as much sense as, well, not being allowed to put coins in your ears in Hawaii. Lots of these silly old laws sit on the state books, and while they haven't been officially abolished, most of them have been forgotten, and today they have no bearing on people's lives whatsoever.

A set of really old laws appears in the Bible, and a lot of people have forgotten about them. Some who haven't forgotten them seem to think the laws don't have any bearing on people today. The laws are known as the Ten Commandments. Several thousand years ago, God wrote them down and gave them to a man named Moses, who then presented the laws to God's chosen people. "So [Moses] was there with the Lord forty days and forty nights. He neither ate bread nor drank water. And

The Law of God

he wrote on the tablets the words of the covenant, the Ten Commandments" (Exodus 34:28).

The Ten Commandments, listed in Exodus 20, describe the best relationship with God and our best relationships with each other. They cover everything from worship to lying—the instruction manual for life. They express God's love, value, and purposes for His people. And in the New Testament Jesus affirms that God's law is still in effect. He said, " 'Do not think that I have come to abolish the Law or the Prophets; I have not come to abolish them but to fulfill them. For truly, I say to you, until heaven and earth pass away, not an iota, not a dot, will pass from the Law until all is accomplished. Therefore whoever relaxes one of the least of these commandments and teaches others to do the same will be called least in the kingdom of heaven, but whoever does them and teaches them will be called great in the kingdom of heaven' " (Matthew 5:17–19). If Jesus still thinks the commandments are important, I suspect He wants those who follow Him to think they are important as well.

But when it comes right down to it, most people don't like to be told what to do. Because the commandments tell us so much about how to live, some people feel as though the laws infringe on their personal freedoms. Why should anybody tell us what to do? Because a life without laws is frightening, not to mention dangerous.

> *Seriously, wouldn't we just figure it out on our own without God telling us what to do?*

The closest thing I ever saw to sheer lawlessness would have to be on the sledding hills that I played on as a kid in Minnesota. A bunch of us kids with instruments of speed careening semi-out-of-control down a hill covered with jumps and other sledders, and no parental supervision. Anything was acceptable.

We would stand on our sleds—sometimes on our heads—and see how far we could make it down the hill. Once that got boring, we built ramps that sent us into the stratosphere. And after that got boring, we began lining each other up to see if we could jump over two, three, or even four bodies. It was awesome. There were so many injuries and wrecks on the hill that we began offering awards such as "Crash of the Day" and "Most Painful-Looking Accident." It is a miracle with all our innovations and cutting-edge sled experimentation that we didn't give someone a broken neck. Now, can you imagine if we had that sort of free-for-all attitude in *every* part of life?

Imagine having people drive their cars everywhere at any time they wanted to—no stoplights or traffic laws at all. Besides inventing all sorts of new shortcuts, people would be in all sorts of car accidents.

And what about having no criminal laws? Imagine a world where people were free to kill, steal, and destroy things at will. No one would be safe. Anytime someone got mad they could pull out a gun and shoot people; anytime someone wanted something they could just take it. Society wouldn't last long, and you probably wouldn't want to live in it. How would your life be different if there were no laws?

Then of course we can't forget the laws of nature God created. Imagine if gravity stopped working right now. You'd fly through your roof and into outer space, which might be cool for a minute, until you suffocated out there among the stars from lack of oxygen. The world spins at something like sixty-seven thousand miles per hour at all times. What if it just stopped all of a sudden? Can you imagine the chaos it would cause? Everything from mountains to trees and buildings would be uprooted and sent flying around in a cataclysmic blur.

As much as we don't like them sometimes, laws aren't a bad thing to have. God decided to give human beings some things they could do in order to have a healthy and happy life here on earth. He even says, " 'And if you faithfully obey the voice of the Lord your God, being careful to do all his commandments that I command you today, the Lord your God will set you high above all the nations of the earth. And all these blessings shall come upon you and overtake you, if you obey the voice of the Lord your God' " (Deuteronomy 28:1, 2).

The simple fact is that laws have consequences. This is a word you've probably heard from your parents on numerous occasions. I know I have. God tells us that when we keep His commandments, blessings will "overtake" us. However, He also says that if we disregard His commandments, things won't be so cheery.

The Law of God

Recently I witnessed a sledding hill accident involving some kids ignoring the most basic of all sledding rules: Don't stand in the middle of the hill. As my wife, a few friends, and I ascended to the sledding hill behind our college a week ago, we were floored by the intelligence deficiency suffered by some on the hill.

First off, the maximum number of sledders this dinky hill could support would probably be in the neighborhood of twenty—not fifty, as was the case that day. An entire throng of snow-tube-toting troublemakers had swarmed the hill like greedy ants after a picnic lunch. Sometimes upwards of twenty-five people, connected together in a train, would go down together, devastating anything in their path.

So I was amazed when I saw a group of kids on either side of the hill jumping in and out of the path of the sledders, thinking themselves clever and quick enough to not get hit. I must confess to you that I found great delight in their daredevilry because I knew what would inevitably happen. I decided to forego the sledding, set my snow tube aside, and sat in the snow in anticipation of some good entertainment.

I didn't have to wait long.

Rocketing down from the top of the hill came my wife of all people, in her tube with a friend, straight toward a fate-tempting child, who had his back turned to the oncoming hill traffic as he pranced around oblivious to the impending doom that awaited him.

It wasn't a dead-on collision, but it was a nice bump. My wife and her friend only clipped him as they flew by; but it was in just the right place. Their snow tube caught his feeble left leg and threw it out from under him. He did a spectacular pirouette and fell face down into the hill. As a concerned adult and pastor I leapt to my feet and cheered for my wife as she completed what I deemed a successful run down the sledding hill and an important lesson taught to a wayward child.

In another crash that day, one boy thought he could jump over an oncoming tube filled with winter thrill-seekers, only to find out that he could fly. The tube hit his feet while he was in midair, which sent him catapulting into the air and spinning a somersault before he slammed back to the ground, where he lay twitching for a few minutes before being carted off the hill. Kids got run over left and right, got bruised and bloodied, and one even ran into my friend Greg's dog, which was chasing after the sledders like she was fetching sticks. It was chaos, and much of it could have been avoided if people had just followed a few little rules of courtesy and common sense.

When we break rules, there are consequences. When it comes to God's laws, we face not only natural consequences, such as getting a bad grade for cheating or losing friends because we are mean to them, but we face eternal consequences as well.

The Bible tells us that God's law is the standard by which we will be judged. It is very clear that refusing to keep God's laws is sin. "Everyone who makes a practice of sinning also practices lawlessness; sin is lawlessness" (1 John 3:4). And the Bible tells us that the cost of sin is death—not a reward in heaven (Romans 6:23).

That is discouraging news to think about, because I have broken God's law sometimes. Who hasn't? The Bible says that *all* have sinned (look at Romans 3:23). The more we study God's laws, the more we realize that we have failed to meet all the requirements. We see this especially when we consider how Jesus summed up the law: " ' "And you shall love the Lord your God with all your heart and with all your soul and with all your mind and with all your strength." The second is this: "You shall love your neighbor as yourself." There is no other commandment greater than these' " (Mark 12:30, 31).

Great. Just great. I mean, are you loving all the time? Do you always love people around you—or do you sometimes wish you could just lock them up in a closet for a while? Do you always share with and sacrifice for those around you? I didn't think so. So what hope is there when the law seems to point out everything we are not?

The answer is Jesus Christ.

One of the functions of the law, besides counseling us on the best way to live and love, is to point out the sin in our lives so we can understand our need for a Savior. Without Jesus coming here to live and die on our behalf, we would be left to do our own good works to obtain salvation and get right with God, which of course we could never do.

"For by grace you have been saved through faith. And this is not your own doing; it is the gift of God, not a result of works, so that no one may boast" (Ephesians 2:8, 9). Grace simply means being given something we don't deserve; and through His death Jesus gave us the grace we needed to meet the requirements of the law.

This doesn't mean that we just do whatever we want because Jesus gives us grace (look up Romans 6:1, 2); on the contrary, grace encourages us and empowers us to fulfill the law. And anyone who claims to follow Christ will be given strength—through the Holy Spirit—to fulfill the law, which is simply loving God and loving each other. "Therefore love is the fulfilling of the law" (Romans 13:10).

Having this type of love for God and man proves that you are a follower of Christ. Jesus said that people would know who His followers were by how they loved one another (see John 13:35). Think of it this way. If I claim to love my wife but pull her hair every time I see her, she will probably come to the conclusion that I don't love her that much. If you claim to study really hard but you fail all your classes, then there is a good chance you should quit playing videogames and crack open a book or two. So when we say that we are followers of Jesus but don't keep His commandments, there is a good chance we are following somebody else.

In a way, God's Ten Commandments are like Ten Freedoms, because when I keep them I don't have to worry about all the stress and mess that not following them could bring into my life. It makes me wonder why anyone wouldn't want to follow God's law. God wants us to live happy lives representing Him on this earth. He has given us commandments so we can avoid getting into trouble both here and in the life to come when Jesus returns.

As I begin to understand God's laws I see that even though they are old, they have a great deal of importance in how I live my life now, and they are worth following. Not following them would be crazier than citizens not being allowed to wear a chicken on their head when they go to Wisconsin.

20 | The Sabbath

The best nap I ever had was in church. I realize that I shouldn't be telling you this, and somewhere a parent may get angry; but the fact is, I have never, ever slumbered so well as I did that Saturday morning in the sanctuary in Minnesota several years ago.

I was your age then and had spent all day Friday traveling up north to visit relatives for a long weekend. After getting in late and talking with the kinfolk till even later, I only managed a few hours of sleep before it was time to rise and shine and give God the glory.

I woke up dazed and confused and stumbled into the bathroom, then into my suit, then out into the car. The drive was so soothing, and I wanted to sleep so badly. But I knew I had to be strong, so I held out until we arrived at church. It was at church, however, that I couldn't hold on any longer.

I'm not sure who spoke at church that day, but their voice had a certain numbing effect on the mind, and it wasn't long before I began losing the battle to stay awake. I gently leaned my head back, resting it on the back of the fourth pew from the front, and fell into a deep sleep. I don't know what I dreamed about that fateful Saturday morning, but

The Sabbath

as I was coming to, I kept hearing this snorting and heavy breathing, and it seemed to be getting louder. Finally it got so loud I had to open my eyes and take a look around to see what was making that terrible ruckus. I sat up with a jolt and looked behind me. There was no more noise, but my eyes met the stares of several pious churchgoers who looked as though they had eaten something sour. I turned and faced forward again, and that's when it dawned on me.

I had been woken by my own snoring.

By the looks of things, I had been out for a while. I heard the minister announce the closing hymn, and I saw the longest strand of drool going from my chin to a little pool in my lap. I'm surprised I didn't drown in it. It was a little embarrassing to say the least; but at least I felt rested!

The Bible tells us that Saturday—the seventh day of the week—is a day of rest.

"And on the seventh day God finished his work that he had done, and he rested on the seventh day from all his work that he had done" (Genesis 2:2). This special day of the week was designed to give people a break and focus on what really matters. It was a day set aside from every other day of the week and was especially blessed by God. The Bible says, "So God blessed the seventh day and made it holy, because on it God rested from all his work that he had done in creation" (Genesis 2:3). But God's purpose for creating Saturday wasn't just a weekly nap; it has a much greater purpose.

In 1982, after much fund-raising and hard work, the Vietnam War Memorial was completed in Washington, D.C. The huge wall contains the names of more than fifty-eight thousand men and women who died or went missing in that awful battle. It is a symbol to their courage and strength and serves a very important function for those of us who did not participate in the war directly.

The memorial is a reminder. When you look at each name, you are reminded that a living, breathing person like you faced danger head-on and made a sacrifice that is difficult to comprehend. When we look at the entire glossy black stone, with thousands of silver names etched into it, we begin to understand how costly and painful war is.

What We Believe

Memorials like this one serve to impress in our minds that our freedom in America isn't free and that war is always ugly. Memorials are important because people tend to be forgetful—even of important things.

One of the reasons God set Saturday apart and blessed it was to serve as a memorial to creation. It is the only commandment that has the word *remember* in it.

" 'Remember the Sabbath day, to keep it holy. Six days you shall labor, and do all your work, but the seventh day is a Sabbath to the Lord your God. On it you shall not do any work, you, or your son, or your daughter, your male servant, or your female servant, or your livestock, or the sojourner who is within your gates. For in six days the Lord made heaven and earth, the sea, and all that is in them, and rested the seventh day. Therefore the Lord blessed the Sabbath day and made it holy' " (Exodus 20:8–11).

We live in a world where people are forgetting where they came from. Most people hold to theories about evolution and the universe resulting from a huge explosion. But the Bible says something entirely different. Even though the Bible is clear on the fact that God is Creator, people still forget—even some people who claim to be Christians. This is why God instituted the Sabbath, to remind us of where we came from and who is in charge. Because it's so important, God has commanded that nobody do any work that day so we can have time to reflect on what He has done for us and worship Him. It's a holy day off—a holiday of sorts.

One of the strangest holidays in the world, at least for someone in America, has to be Guy Fawkes Night. It is a holiday marking the prevention of a group of local terrorists from blowing up the British Parliament in the 1600s. This group was unhappy with the government, to put it mildly. While a number of people were involved in carting thirty-six barrels of gunpowder into the basement of Parliament, many of them realized that innocent people would be injured or killed in their attempt to send a message to the royal family. So many of them backed out—and one of them squealed via a letter that made its way into the king's hands. However, no one told poor Guy Fawkes.

The Sabbath

So, in the wee morning hours of November 5, troops stormed the Parliament basement and found Fawkes there with thirty-six barrels of gunpowder. Bummer. He was caught, tortured, and executed. And because Parliament was saved from a terrible misfortune by routing out the terrorists, people observe Guy Fawkes Night in Britain.

To celebrate, people light bonfires and put likenesses of Guy Fawkes atop them. How's that for a gruesomely strange celebration?

The Sabbath can be tricky for a lot of people to observe because they aren't sure exactly what to do during a celebration of Creation. It can be as strange as Guy Fawkes Night. So, if you are one of those people wondering how you can celebrate this special day—be at peace. The Bible points out that this holy day doesn't require anything too strange—at least no bonfires with human likenesses.

The Bible gives us a few guidelines for observing the Sabbath. The first is when it starts. Days were reckoned a little differently in Bible times. Each day began at sundown and ended at sunset the next evening. This means the biblical Sabbath begins Friday night at sundown and ends at sundown Saturday night.

The next thing to know is the most obvious—don't work on that day. Work is stressful and something you have to do most days of the week; and even if you don't have a job, you have homework. To keep the Sabbath, it is important to put away everything we do during the week that could be considered work; that way you have time to reflect on and remember God as Creator. It's a good idea to shut off the TV and put away secular music on the Sabbath so our thoughts can focus on spiritual things, instead of all the other stuff we think about during the week. The Bible tells us to keep Sabbath holy, which means to keep it set apart from other days. It's nice to do something different on God's special day that involves Him.

The third thing to do is to remember the Sabbath day by what we spend our time doing instead of work. Now I know the commandment says we need to rest, and believe me, I think there are Sabbaths when the best thing you can do is sleep because you have had such a rough week and need to recuperate. However, there are more ways to rest from work than literally snoozing the day away. We can do a lot more than be vegetables on the Sabbath, and Jesus shows us how.

What We Believe

The religious leaders of Jesus' day had a problem knowing what to do on the Sabbath—they just thought it was important to know what you couldn't do. They made up hundreds of "don'ts" for the Sabbath, and as a result the day became a terrible burden instead of a holy celebration. This is a mistake people still make today. But God's Sabbath isn't supposed to be a day of limitations; it's a day of celebration, freedom, and remembrance.

Jesus points out that " 'it is lawful to do good on the Sabbath' " (Matthew 12:12, NIV). He said this as He was healing and helping people. We can do things on the Sabbath that bring God glory and follow Jesus' example to help those in need around us. You can visit a lonely elderly soul in a nursing home, or invite over for lunch some new church members who don't know a lot of people. The possibilities are endless. Serving and helping others on Sabbath is always a great choice.

Another example Jesus left us for observing the Sabbath is attending church. "He went to Nazareth, where he had been brought up, and on the Sabbath day he went into the synagogue, as was his custom" (Luke 4:16, NIV). Seventh-day Adventists and many other Christians recognize Sabbath as the perfect day to worship God in church because after all, it is a day for remembering Him as Creator. What better way to remember God as Creator than to worship Him?

Finally, another way we can honor God's Sabbath is by spending time with family and friends. Human beings are a part of God's creation, and our friends and families are gifts from Him. Sabbath is the perfect day to share a meal with them or go for a walk in the park and really build up our relationships. Jesus spent His Sabbaths with His disciples (close friends) and family as well as with those in need.

God's Sabbath is a wonderful blessing. I can't tell you how many times I have welcomed it with open arms after a hard week of work or study. There is a peace that comes with sundown Friday nights and a joy that comes with worshiping God with family and friends.

A lot of people will tell you that God's Sabbath was just some old Jewish law and keeping it today is a legalistic drudgery, and they will actually feel sorry for people who observe God's seventh-day Sabbath.

The Sabbath

They'll tell you that Sabbath can be any day you want it to be and that it doesn't matter when you worship God.

Well, they are right that we can worship God on any day—and we should. But if they looked honestly at their Bibles, they would see that nowhere in Scripture does God name any other day of the week as a special day like Sabbath. They would see that the seventh-day Sabbath was a memorial instituted at Creation and applies to all human beings at all times, not just one group here or there. And as far as Sabbath being a pain to observe—that all depends on what you make it out to be.

If you approach Sabbath as a day of "dos" and "don'ts" or only a day to take a nap on, then, yes, it becomes like any other day—and even annoying because of its restrictions. But if you keep it as the Bible says, then you will find the Sabbath to be anything but a pain. It will be a day you welcome every week with great anticipation and joy because it gives you a chance to reconnect with God and loved ones—and that's something you won't want to sleep through.

21 | Stewardship

One of the most traumatic moments of my life occurred on the monkey bars when I was in kindergarten. I was happily climbing this wall made of blue bars that rose about ten feet in the air. On the other side were all my little kindergarten friends waiting for my arrival so we could hit up the slide and the swings. However, we kindergartners weren't the only ones on the playground that afternoon. The fourth-graders were lurking about, and it didn't take long for one of them to find us. When he did, it resulted in a battle for my very life.

He was huge. Abnormally huge for a fourth-grader. He could have passed for a high-schooler, and maybe he was supposed to be but just couldn't pass fourth-grade math. He took one look at me and thought he'd have a little fun. He grabbed my foot and began pulling me off the monkey bars.

Can you imagine what kind of twisted kid would pull a kindergartner off the monkey bars to fall five or six feet to the ground? My friends began hollering and yelling from the other side of the wall as they gazed in horror at the scene, but none of them were brave enough to do anything. I fought and struggled as best I could to get my foot away from this fat fourth-grader, but to no avail. I was beginning to lose my grip.

Suddenly an idea struck me. It was reminiscent of the Bible text that says, "It is more blessed to give than to receive."

If this kid wants my foot so bad, why not just let him have it?

So, I stopped trying to pull my foot away from his grip and relaxed my leg. The result was astounding. Because the kid no longer met resistance from my leg, the force of his own pulling yanked the heel of my foot right into his own face.

Thwack!

Instantly he let go and toppled backwards to the ground, covering his face. Swiftly I raced over the top of the monkey bar wall, to the adulation of my peers, while the fourth-grader ran off crying to get sympathy from his teacher.

Freedom comes with giving, and not just when it comes to your feet and large fourth-graders. God really does tell us that when we give we are more blessed—or happy—than when we receive. He should know, since He has given us everything.

God has given us everything from the breath of life in our nostrils (Genesis 2:7) to our money (Psalm 50:12) to our gifts and abilities that help us succeed at work and sharing His message of love to the world (1 Corinthians 12:4). Right from the beginning, just after Creation, God said, " 'Prosper! Reproduce! Fill Earth! Take charge! Be responsible for fish in the sea and birds in the air, for every living thing that moves on the face of the Earth' " (Genesis 1:28, *The Message*). God has given people everything in the earth to take care of, not a small responsibility by any means.

To sum this up: Everything belongs to God. Yet He has given us everything, even His own Son, Jesus, to save us from death. How can we respond to such generosity? No card is big enough to contain all the words of appreciation needed to thank God. No gift we could ever give would match what God has granted us.

David expressed this same idea when he wrote, " 'But who am I, and what is my people, that we should be able thus to offer willingly? For all things come from you' " (1 Chronicles 29:14). David is flustered because

What We Believe

God's gifts are so overwhelming, and even if he gives back to God, whatever he gives belonged to God anyway. So what can we do? God gives us a way we can demonstrate how thankful we are for His provision in our lives.

In the passage in Genesis where God gives the earth to man, we get a glimpse into what God expects us to do. He tells Adam to "be responsible" for the earth. In other passages we see Jesus telling stories about managing things responsibly, so that if you are faithful with what you have, you will be given even more (look up Luke 16). It all points to the idea that we are to be responsible to manage God's things in a way that would make Him happy. This is called being a steward. But sometimes it is easier said than done.

Recently I was in a thrift shop snooping around the book section when I stumbled upon a brand-new college textbook. College textbooks are *very* expensive items, and here sat a brand-new, unmarked copy of a business text that someone had carelessly dumped off at the thrift shop. I quickly bought it for the princely sum of one—count it—one dollar. The very same day I sold it online for fifty bucks. The name of the textbook?

Investments.

Besides knowing there is a business student out there with a very bleak future in the world of investment, we are given a lesson in how easy it is to be careless with our stuff. We tend to be a society of wasters. We waste everything. The statistics are frightening. In the United States alone we waste roughly ninety-six billion pounds of food each year. That's enough to feed a quarter of the world's population for a year, not including the United States.

Another big thing we waste is our time. I don't know how many times I have come to the end of the week and asked myself, "What did I do all week?" It's not that I wasn't busy—I was—but sometimes I have nothing to show for it. We miss so many chances to do awesome things for God and develop the abilities He has given us because we just plain get distracted by other things.

On the flipside, sometimes we are so busy we forget to enjoy some distractions from work once in a while to give ourselves a rest. Perhaps

Stewardship

the most dangerous misuse of our time is when we forget to talk to God and spend time listening to Him.

Another gift God has given us that we are careless with is our money. I don't know how many times I have bought stuff I didn't need and forgot I even wanted a couple months later. Then there is the fact that about 43 percent of families spend more money than they make each year and owe about eight thousand dollars just on their credit cards. And that debt is most likely not from giving to needy people and charities.

God did not design us to be wasters. He wants us to be good stewards. And while it can be a struggle to break bad habits when we are used to being disorganized and careless, some great benefits come with being more careful with what God has given us. It's really a privilege when you think about it.

> *What area of your life do you think you waste too much in?*

In the Bible God tells us that if we " 'seek first the kingdom of God and his righteousness . . . all these things will be added to you' " (Matthew 6:33). God tells us that if we are careful to do what He wants first, He will make sure the rest of our life is taken care of.

A long time ago one of my college professors told me that God has a "circle of blessing," which simply means that when we trust God with our stuff, He will be sure to bless us even more. For example, if I become intentional and plan time with God as well as time to develop the abilities He has given me, He will open more doors for me to use what I have learned in new and exciting ways. It also means I won't be as stressed out because if I'm careful with my time, I won't procrastinate doing my homework to the last minute (something I'm a master at). When we use our time and talents for God, it brings us into a closer relationship with Him, who gives us courage and hope as we face the challenges that life throws at us every day.

And then there is our money. God has given special instructions for how we are to be stewards of the finances He gives us. He tells us to "Bring the full tithes into the storehouse, that there may be food in my house. And thereby put me to the test, says the Lord of hosts, if I will not open the windows of heaven for you and pour down for you a blessing until there is no more need" (Malachi 3:10). Tithe was something God started way back before Abraham and has called us to do as well.

Tithing simply means giving the first tenth of whatever you have to God. Now, we don't do this because God needs our money. Remember, He's the One who gives it in the first place. Tithe accomplishes two things. First, it provides finances that help people minister the gospel around the world. Second, it reminds us that we owe God everything and that we are simply managers of what we are given. It is a way for us to tell God that we know where our blessings come from and a way for us to trust Him instead of thinking we are self-sufficient with the money we make.

Also we find people in the Bible frequently giving God an offering. This is money above and beyond the required 10 percent that we give as tithe. Offerings are given to God as expressions of thanks, as a way to spread the gospel (like the tithe), or as a way to meet the physical needs of those people hurting around us. God promises that anyone who "sows sparingly will also reap sparingly, and whoever sows generously will also reap generously" (2 Corinthians 9:6, NIV). In other words, when we are generous with our acknowledgment of God, He is generous toward us.

When I was seventeen I had a chance to play on a CD recording with a Christian band in my youth group. I was so excited I could hardly focus on anything as the day of the live concert recording approached. But as the day drew near I became aware of a problem. The amplifier I was using for my electric guitar was sorely underpowered for the job. It didn't sound the best and would affect the recording. At first it didn't look as though I would be a part of this project, since the type of amplifier I needed was really expensive.

Then one evening as I was dragging my feet into the worship service, feeling totally hopeless, God impressed me to give twenty bucks in the offering plate. The problem was that all the money I had in the world amounted to twenty bucks. God was asking me to give an offering right smack in the middle of a time when I *needed* money.

Stewardship

I tried to ignore the prompting of the Holy Spirit on my heart all evening, but when the offering plate came around I couldn't deny it. I had to give in. I put my last twenty bucks in the plate—but I wasn't happy about it. I couldn't focus all through the service. I didn't understand why I had to give that dumb offering. I didn't understand until the end of the service.

My friend Daryl, a musician I played with occasionally, came up to me as I was leaving the sanctuary and said, "Hey, Seth! Come with me. I have something for you!" I followed him out to his truck, where he proceeded to unload the type of amplifier I so desperately needed.

"For you," he said.

I didn't know how to respond, except to praise God that He was telling the truth in the Bible. Since then, I have been blessed numerous times as I have been faithful with my tithes and offerings. God has come through for me in so many ways that I would need to write another book just to list half of them. And I don't give God my time and money just so I can get stuff; rather, I trust Him with it, and I know that ultimately everything I get belongs to Him anyway.

The Bible says, " 'Give, and it will be given to you. Good measure, pressed down, shaken together, running over, will be put into your lap. For with the measure you use it will be measured back to you' " (Luke 6:38). And the Bible goes on to say, "And my God will supply every need of yours according to his riches in glory in Christ Jesus" (Philippians 4:19).

God has promised that when we are willing to give to Him and not resist, He can't resist giving to us. When we trust Him with everything we have, He will entrust us with more and more. When we are faithful to invest in Him, He will invest more in us. There is no fourth-grade bully big enough to stop God from blessing His faithful stewards.

22 | Christian Behavior

You can make yourself get up early in the morning in many ways. You can set your alarm clock, go to bed at a decent hour, or have someone who regularly gets up early call you or tap you on the head repeatedly when they get up. But there is one sure-fire method to make yourself get out of bed early that you should never attempt because it's never a positive experience. Believe me when I tell you: Never *ever* eat Taco Bell after midnight.

My second year in college I learned this important life lesson the hard way. I had a friend who worked at Taco Bell, and every night at the end of his shift he would offer to bring us back the free food of our choice. This was a ray of sunshine from heaven, as most college kids are so poor they would rejoice over being offered a free cardboard sandwich.

On one particular evening I had placed an order for two chili cheese burritos. After midnight, two chili cheese burritos are two too many. About six hours later I woke up to a very special experience that will be forever etched into my memory.

Around 6:00 A.M. something began to stir. Actually, "bubble" is probably a better word. It didn't take long before my natural alarm clock, located in my intestines, told me that it was time to get up. And then my survival instinct told me I had better get to the bathroom.

Whatever evil was brewing in my body hit my innards like ocean waves smacking into a sandcastle. It heaved and swelled in my gut until it brought tears to my eyes and I had to roll out of bed. And I mean that literally. The pain was so debilitating that I had to roll off the bed onto all fours. Not an impressive dismount by any means, but style and form are not a consideration when you have more gas in your body than in your car.

I began crawling toward that special sanctuary for the suffering and let out a groan of agony. My roommate woke up and saw my crumpled form moving very slowly across the floor.

"Dude, are you OK?"

"Oh . . . yeah," I whimpered between gasps for precious air. "Just . . . going to the bathroom . . . trying not to die on the way there."

That horrible trip reminded me of those people who get stranded in the desert and they are all torn up and ragged as they crawl hopefully toward an oasis for water. Eventually I made it, and that's when the pain really flared up. I don't know how long I pondered life on that piece of porcelain, but it was long enough to see my life flash before my eyes.

When that part of the crisis was over, I lay on the cool tile floor of the bathroom and said a little one-sentence prayer over and over again.

"Please, don't let me die like this."

After forty-five minutes or so, the painful swelling of who-knows-what in my body died down, and I was able to stagger back to my bed, where I had one of the more restful sleeps of my life. And when the rude awakening happened again at 8:00 A.M., I knew two things. One, that I needed to get back to the bathroom for more pondering, and two, I would never eat Taco Bell that late again.

Some choices we make in life really give us a miserable time, even worse than a chili cheese burrito after midnight. Newton's third law states that for every action there is an equal or opposite reaction. In the same vein as that law is the idea that for every choice we make there are consequences. That is why the Bible is full of principles to live by, ranging from diet to decision making, to help us live the happiest and most successful life possible. The disciple John wrote, "Dear friend, I pray that you may enjoy good health and that all may go well with you, even as your soul is getting along well" (3 John 1:2, NIV). So why is God so concerned about how we behave and the choices we make?

The first reason has to do with the quality of our life now. Jesus said, " 'I came that they may have life and have it abundantly' " (John 10:10). That's not just talking about life in heaven—it's talking about life now. This is a fairly easy reason to understand. If Jesus spent all sorts of time telling us in His Word how much He loves us but gave us no instruction or promises to help us live better lives on earth, we probably wouldn't think He was as loving as He said He was. How would you like a God who said, "You know, when you get to heaven everything will be perfect; but while you're here I can't help you." That'd be pretty lame, wouldn't it? But there are two more reasons that have an even greater effect on us than our perception of God.

Our relationship with God can be affected drastically by how we live our life. The Bible tells us "whoever says he abides in him ought to walk in the same way in which he walked" (1 John 2:6). So we are called to walk as Jesus walked, meaning to live life as He did. This is done partly to influence others (which we will talk about shortly) but also to protect our relationship with God. Let me give you an example.

I read the story of a man who was about to cheat on his wife, and he asked a Christian friend whether God could forgive him or not if he did it. The Christian thought for a while. He knew God could forgive anything, but he was afraid that if he told his friend this truth, the friend would use God's grace as a license (permission) to sin, something the Bible strongly forbids. Thankfully, the Christian came up with a very insightful answer and said, "Yes, God can give you forgiveness—but you may not want it."

Unfortunately this proved true, as the guy decided to cheat on his wife and then got a divorce. When his Christian friend confronted him about his behavior and God's ability to forgive and heal, the guy who had cheated refused God. He said he didn't want or need God anymore. What happened? The man lived his life in a way that took him further from God, and as a result, he lost his relationship with Jesus and didn't even miss it.

Now I believe it takes a lot to move someone that far away from God. God is so gracious and tries everything He can to get our attention. But when we persist in harmful behaviors it gets harder and harder for us to notice God and His love reaching out to us. Some obvious bad behaviors are things like drug abuse, violence, and stealing. Those illegal activities have a way of corrupting our values and even altering our minds. When our values and ways of thinking are the opposite of God's, it's harder for us to want Him to change us. Not to mention that the more we allow ourselves to do things contrary to God's Word, the more we get used to taking orders from ourselves instead of letting God lead our lives.

Some not-so-obvious ways we can act may lead us away from our relationship with God. Things like eating an unhealthy diet, using foul language, listening to music that promotes things the Bible condemns, and spending too much money on stuff we don't need can have a negative effect on our relationship with God. Think about it. If you eat foods that make your body really sick you might have a hard time giving God praise and glory because your life is so miserable. A lot of people blame God for their sickness when in fact if they had been a little more careful with what they crammed into their mouth or been more proactive about exercise they might feel better and be able to praise God for the health principles in His Word. "So, whether you eat or drink, or whatever you do, do all to the glory of God" (1 Corinthians 10:31). It's mighty hard to give God any glory when you are doubled up on the bathroom floor wishing you hadn't even looked at a chili cheese burrito.

If you become obsessed with spending money on all the stuff you can get your hands on, it is possible that getting more stuff will become the focus of your life and where you get your values, as opposed to serving God and getting your values from Him. We can easily let our possessions "possess" us instead of giving our lives to God. "Do not let your adorning be external—the braiding of hair, the wearing of gold, or the

What We Believe

putting on of clothing" (1 Peter 3:3). The Bible isn't saying we can't have nice things, or enjoy the best quality, or look nice, but it is saying that we need to be careful that what we buy doesn't end up owning us and our hearts.

Finally, how we live our life has a great deal of influence on other people and how we represent God to them. An old bumper sticker says, "Jesus, please save me from Your followers." It makes some sense, unfortunately. A lot of people who claim to be Christians don't behave like Christians. Not just in what they eat, buy, or do, but in their character as well. The Bible tells us that " 'all men will know that you are my disciples, if you love one another' " (John 13:35). Christians are called to have a loving character, but sometimes we have a reputation for being judgmental, hypocritical, and not accepting. As a result, people are turned off to God and His ways.

Our behavior affects other Christians too. "But take care that this right of yours does not somehow become a stumbling block to the weak" (1 Corinthians 8:9). The way we act can cause other people to struggle in their relationship with God. For example, if a Christian gets it in his head that he should watch a movie filled with all sorts of graphic violence and crass language, another Christian who might not know better could say, "Hey if *he* is doing it, why can't I?" Or if a physically attractive Christian dresses in a way that's revealing and suggestive, she could cause another Christian to start having less than holy thoughts about her or what he would like to do with her. If we cause others to stumble over our behavior, we can influence them to move away from what God wants for their life.

Now sometimes people will stumble no matter what we do, because in this world we have misunderstandings and personal weaknesses. But the idea is for us not to cause them any undue stumbling. We are to lift each other up and help each other to get closer to God.

We are called to live our lives in a way that demonstrates health, love, and connectedness to God. "Therefore, we are ambassadors for Christ, God making his appeal through us. We implore you on behalf of Christ, be reconciled to God" (2 Corinthians 5:20). Christians' behavior has everything to do with representing Christ to the world, to let

Him guide what we eat and how we dress all the way down to how we worship God in our personal life and how we love others. We are walking witnesses for Jesus—one of heaven's most powerful and influential weapons against the devil and the darkness of sin.

We are visible to everyone. " 'You are the light of the world. A city set on a hill cannot be hidden' " (Matthew 5:14). And the Bible calls us " 'the salt of the earth' " (Matthew 5:13, NIV). This means that we season the earth by the way we live, to, as *The Message* Bible puts it, bring out the "God-flavors" in the earth. We help people "Taste and see that the Lord is good" (Psalm 34:8, NIV). God's way is one we can experience and "taste," even after midnight, with no rude awakenings.

23 | Marriage and the Family

Today I came across a bizarre story about a man, his dog, and their wedding. That's right—their (man + dog) wedding. An elderly man from Nepal, seventy-five years of age, married a dog in a local custom to ensure good luck. His son, his friends, and other relatives by his side, Phulram Chaudhary wedded a dog in Durgauli village in the southwestern Kailali district.

The man was following a custom of his community. The custom holds that an old man who regrows teeth must take a dog to be his "lawfully wedded wife." Personally I think I'd be happy living with dentures rather than a dog-wife. And I hope this guy didn't have to "kiss the bride," because it would have all been in vain as well as utter grossness.

Why in vain, do you say? Didn't he have any luck for all his efforts? Well, read for yourself. According to the local paper, "He believed that this would help him avoid great misfortune later in life. However, he died a few days afterward." Such a shame, and now the dog is a widow.

People have a lot of confusion about what defines a marriage these days. If you check the news, you can see any variety of combinations of life forms united in wedlock; if you look a little harder, you can even see marriages between people and inanimate objects. I recently read of one man who, in order to be closer to God, married a shrine—not exactly the most affectionate or talkative spouse one could have. Today people are talking back and forth, sometimes very hatefully, about what a marriage is. Thankfully we have a picture in the Bible of what marriage was originally designed and purposed to be.

It happened back in Eden in a lovely garden ceremony, when God created the first woman and introduced her to the first man. "And the rib that the Lord God had taken from the man he made into a woman and brought her to the man. Then the man said, 'This at last is bone of my bones and flesh of my flesh; she shall be called Woman because, she was taken out of Man' " (Genesis 2:22, 23).

Eve was presented to Adam, and Adam was so delighted that he composed a little poem in her honor. Just in case we think this is one scenario out of a multitude of different types of marriage unions, the Bible says, "Therefore a man shall leave his father and his mother and hold fast to his wife, and they shall become one flesh" (Genesis 2:24). Marriage is the union between one man and one woman. That was how God created it in the beginning. Any other type of union happened after sin entered the world.

This doesn't mean a union between a man and a woman is perfect. The entry of sin into the world took its toll on the harmony of godly marriages. So while marriage is still the unity of two people, they don't always have a perfect fit, at least not right away.

In writing of marriage Katharine Hepburn said, "Sometimes I wonder if men and women really suit each other. Perhaps they should live next door and just visit now and then." This comment is obviously coming from someone who has either experienced a difficult marriage or seen other people having a hard time of it. Troubled marriages are everywhere. I have heard people say as many as half of all marriages end in divorce. While this may be happening for numerous

> *What factors do you think make a marriage healthy or unhealthy?*

reasons, many times it is because the individuals entering into the marriage have not given it much thought or much commitment. So when problems arise because one person likes to do things one way and the other person has a different way, the couple calls it quits. Marriage takes a deep commitment and lots of understanding because two lives are slowly meshing over fifty or sixty years. But it is a tremendous blessing when you enter into it with the right mind-set. A better quote than the one from our friend Katharine says, "What counts in making a happy marriage is not so much how compatible you are, but how you deal with incompatibility" (Leo Tolstoy). And how do we deal with incompatibility?

What do we do when one person goes to bed late and wakes up the person who went to bed early by boisterously readjusting the blankets? Is there any hope for commitment when someone lazily leaves the dishes undone for the other spouse to enjoy? And is there any chance when the man leaves the toilet seat up? Absolutely.

Even more important than love, commitment, and understanding, the first step is to base a marriage on a relationship to God. The Bible says, "Do not be yoked together with unbelievers. For what do righteousness and wickedness have in common? Or what fellowship can light have with darkness?" (2 Corinthians 6:14, NIV). Basically this is saying don't be connected in the deepest parts of your heart to someone who doesn't believe in God. It's not that we can't be friends with nonbelievers or that God doesn't love them as much as He loves the Christian. It's just that God knows that when two people get together and have major rifts over their beliefs, life and love are a lot tougher in the long run. If both individuals love God, when the positive traits of the relationship become weakened by anger, stress, and miscommunications, God's grace can work on their hearts. He is the One who holds things together in hard times.

> *Even though we understand it's not best to be united with someone who has a different faith, what do you think makes Christians marry non-Christians anyway?*

Marriage and the Family

Most important, God shapes and molds the characters of those in the marriage so that if they have kids, the children will have a positive influence—something we have less and less of in the world.

I have worked in various forms of youth ministry for several years, and I can tell you the greatest asset to a youth ministry is the parents, but they can also be the greatest hindrance. For example, if kids come to a Christian summer camp and make a decision to follow Jesus, it has the potential to change their life forever for the better. And if they go home to a loving family, with parents who respect and nurture their child's decision to follow Jesus, those children have a tremendous chance of following Jesus the rest of their lives and becoming powerful leaders for Him.

On the other hand, if the kids make a decision for God and then go home to parents who are critical of faith and show no love for God or each other, there is a problem. The kids might have an hour or two of spiritual encouragement at church every week, but they spend all the rest of the time in an environment that tries to kill their faith.

A marriage between a godly man and woman is one of the ways God uses to save and shape children. When it is formed correctly with love, understanding, and a commitment to God, the resulting family provides one of the greatest tools of God's kingdom for reaching the lost.

How does it do that? When people think of an ideal family, they see a group of people loving and accepting each other no matter what. The group may not be perfect (no family is, and I bet yours is just as weird as mine), but they stick together through it all. Godly families share their lives and a commitment to each other that seeks to help each family member grow into all that God can make them to be. This is what church should strive to be—a church family.

When nonbelievers encounter a family rich with God's love, they see a microcosm (mini version) of the church. Seeing how Christians love and interact with each other has a powerful impact on them, because not everyone has that kind of love in their life, and most people wish for it. As a Christian family embraces nonbelievers into their lives, they can point the people to Christ. When nonbelievers begin to see Christ, they will realize that while they cannot formally join another earthly family, they *can* join God's family, which is the church. By doing so, not only will they have a new family, but they will also be a part of the greatest marriage of all. It's the marriage that happens when Jesus (the Groom) returns to claim the church (His bride) and take her home to live with Him forever in perfect love and unity.

" 'Therefore a man shall leave his father and mother and hold fast to his wife, and the two shall become one flesh.' This mystery is profound, and I am saying that it refers to Christ and the church" (Ephesians 5:31, 32).

24 | Christ's Ministry in the Heavenly Sanctuary

Late one night a couple of years ago, I was driving home on a stretch of road in the huge metropolis of Abilene, Kansas (population 6,500). I was on the main street heading out of town when out of the neighborhood on my left side dashed an orange striped cat. It leaped into the road and stopped—stunned—right in front of my little Saturn sedan. I scarcely had time to think, much less react to the furry feline stalled in the path of my automobile traveling at forty miles per hour. I couldn't swerve to my right because I would hit another car, and I couldn't very well go to my left because I'd have a head-on collision with oncoming traffic. The only thing I could do was hope that this encounter would be like those animal miracle stories you read about in some books or hear about on the radio or the news.

You know the kind—the ones where an animal is in peril, trapped under an old abandoned house, or stuck on the railroad tracks, or standing in the way of an oncoming burgundy Saturn in Abilene, Kansas, and at the last minute an angel swoops down and takes the sweet critter off to a safe place or to heaven. Yeah . . . yeah! Maybe this was going to

What We Believe

be something I could share during children's story about how God cares about even our pets and—

KA-KLUNK!

Nope, not going to be one of those stories. For a moment, as the awful sound sank into my soul and I felt a sickening horror seep into my heart, I thought maybe the cat would be all right. The story could still have a good ending, right? Maybe the cat would have a broken leg or two, but it would be nursed back to health by an orphan who needed a friend; or maybe the cat would be missing an eye or an ear but still be able to rescue a drowning kid in a river or sing the national anthem or . . . then I looked in the rearview mirror.

I think the image of that furry little friend's body tumbling and flopping toward the wheels of the car behind me will haunt me to my dying day. It certainly haunted me for the next several nights as I had nightmares about it. That horrid image is still burned into my memory, and now it's burned into yours. No, no need to thank me. Just pay attention.

Imagine having to hit a poor defenseless animal like this every time you messed up in life. Seriously. Imagine that every time you sinned you had to intentionally run over a kitten or a puppy. (Yeah, I know, this is turning out to be the most uplifting chapter of all time, but just hang in there—we are just going to take this one step further.) Imagine that the animal you had to intentionally kill wasn't a stray but your beloved pet—the same one you take care of, love, and play with. Picture having to kill a pet every single time you sinned. You'd probably stop bothering with pets after a while. And as awful as this may seem, if you lived in Old Testament times and you were a follower of God, this is exactly what you'd have to do if you wanted forgiveness.

Before Jesus came and died for our sins and sent us the Holy Spirit to dwell in our hearts and help us on our way, there was the sanctuary system. It involved a huge tent made of ornate metals, woods, and fabrics with several important and fascinating parts—but none so important and fascinating as the Holy and Most Holy Places, which were taken care of by the priests (sort of the equivalent of your pastor today).

Back then, if you sassed your parents, lied, cheated, stole something, or let your bull gore someone (no kidding, it was a problem back then, look it up in Exodus 21:28–32), then you would have to make a sacrifice for your sin. What's more, even if you didn't *mean* to punch your sister in the face and knock her teeth out, you would still have to kill an animal. And not just any animal but the best you had.

The Bible says, " 'If his offering is a burnt offering [a sacrifice, in other words] from the herd, he shall offer a male without blemish. . . . He shall lay his hand on the head of the burnt offering, and it shall be accepted for him to make atonement for him' " (Leviticus 1:3, 4). Atonement is a word that simply means to be made right with God, to have your relationship with Him restored; to be "at one" with Him, hence "at-one-ment." So why would you need to kill something, and what's with the laying-on-of-hands business? It's all about transferring.

I used to work at a job that required me to answer phones and help customers who had different kinds of needs, personalities, and levels of intelligence. Frequently I would get a ringy-dingy from a ding-a-ling whose personality complemented their . . . uh . . . special level of intelligence. It was at these times that I did the most professional thing I could think of: I transferred them to somebody else. One trick I enjoyed playing on my coworkers was to cover the receiver with my hand so the caller couldn't hear and then put on the best fake smile I had and call a coworker over and say, "It's for you!"

Judging by my tone, smile, and the twinkle in my eye (which has taken me years to develop) they would think that it was their boyfriend or girlfriend, a loving parent, or some long-lost pet that was checking in after all these years. They would take the phone excitedly out of my hand and chirp, "Hello?"

By this time I had managed to run all the way out to the parking lot and jump in my car, which I entered, locked, and waited in safety for five to ten minutes while my coworker communicated with the customer who was a few clowns short of a circus. Of course I was glared at when I resumed my post, but any persecution I had to endure was worth it, as one of the most unpleasant experiences in the world is being stuck on the phone with a difficult customer. So what's my point, besides setting a shining example for you to follow at your workplace?

We are stuck with the worst customer of all—sin. According to the Bible, it will kill us unless we find a way to transfer it out of our lives and give it to something or someone else. This was the big idea behind the sacrificial/sanctuary system. When you laid your hands on your sheep, bull, or bird sacrifice, it symbolized your sins being transferred to them. Then things got ugly.

After laying your hands on, let's say, a sheep, you would then have to cradle it in your arms and pull its neck back so the skin was taut. The creature would look at you pleadingly. Then you would take a razor-sharp knife and place it to the throat, and in one swift movement slice it wide open. The sights and sounds accompanying this act would burn themselves in your mind for a long time, especially since you had to do this several times a year. As you sat there with your dead animal covered in blood, the priests would take over.

> *In your opinion, why did God choose such a brutal method to symbolize forgiveness? Is there anything in the Bible that talks about the importance of blood as it relates to forgiveness?*

The priests had two very important jobs. First they would "bring the blood and throw the blood against the sides of the altar that is the entrance of the tent of meeting [sanctuary]" (Leviticus 1:5). Once again the concept of transferring comes up. First your sin would be transferred to the animal, and then the sin of the animal would be transferred to the sanctuary. Now this begs the question, where did the sin that was transferred to the sanctuary run off to? This brings up the second job, which was mainly for the high priest.

Once a year God's people would have a Day of Atonement, when the high priest, and only the high priest, would cleanse the sanctuary from sin. The job involved three elements:

1. A bath for the high priest (Leviticus 16:4)
2. Two goats (16:8)
3. The Most Holy Place (16:16, 17)

Christ's Ministry in the Heavenly Sanctuary

In the Most Holy Place, the presence of God dwelt in such intensity that if anyone besides the high priest entered it, they would die immediately. The high priest would die if he was not properly prepared.

First the high priest would hop in the tub and make sure he was clean so his bells would keep ringing (see fun fact). Then he would sacrifice a bull (that's right, more blood) to make atonement for himself. Following that, the high priest would take the two goats and set them "before the LORD at the entrance to the Tent of Meeting" (Leviticus 16:7, NIV). Next he would "cast lots" (think drawing names out of hat, except the hat was an urn containing inscribed objects for names), and the Lord would use this method to determine which of the goats would be killed for a sin offering (even more blood) and which one would be for "Azazel." There is some debate as to what Azazel means. It is something you would never name a child, because it is thought to denote the devil. It could mean either "one who removes" or "to go away" in Hebrew. The other goat, the sin offering goat, was killed and its blood sprinkled on the veil that separated the Holy Place from the Most Holy Place and on a part of the ark of the covenant (a lovely box that held the stone tablets of the Ten Commandments, Aaron's rod, and the presence of God) called the mercy seat. This blood would make atonement for the sanctuary.

Whew, almost done.

Finally, the high priest would lay his hands on the head of the still-living Azazel goat, symbolizing the transference of all the sins of the people of Israel. Then the goat was taken far out into the wilderness to wander toward a future that was probably no better than for the goat

> **FUN FACT:**
>
> *As a precaution, the high priest had bells around the bottom of his tunic and a rope was tied to his ankle. If the priest was not clean and he had a less-than-happy encounter with the most holy God, his bells would stop jingling, alerting those outside that something was wrong. Then they could drag the body out by the rope tied around the ankle.*

that was sacrificed. This release into the wilderness symbolized the sin being removed from the camp of Israel—and whenever sin is removed there is cause to rejoice.

But after all the sacrificing and copious amounts of blood and ceremony, we must—or at least I must—ask the question, Couldn't God have thought of a better way to remove sin from our lives? The answer is absolutely *yes*.

In Jesus Christ, God offered a better system and a better sacrifice. Jesus was to shed His divine blood—once—and it would be so powerful that it could cover any human being, in any time, in any condition, if they would only accept it. Jesus was willing to have us transfer our sins to Him and be sacrificed so we could be free. And if that wasn't enough, He—not another sinful human being—was to become our High Priest. Look at what the Bible says:

But this one [Jesus] was made a priest with an oath by the one who said to him:

"The Lord has sworn and will not change his mind,
'You are a priest forever.' " . . .

The former priests were many in number, because they were prevented by death from continuing in office, but he holds his priesthood permanently, because he continues forever. Consequently, he is able to save to the uttermost those who draw near to God through him (Hebrews 7:21, 23–25).

After Jesus rose from the dead, He ascended to heaven, where He was made our heavenly High Priest. There He applies His sacrifice/blood that was shed on our behalf to the heavenly sanctuary to atone for our sins. This makes us ask one more question: If the high priest in the Old Testament had a two-phase ministry, where is Christ's second phase? Thankfully, we have some insight via the book of Daniel.

In chapter 8 of this Old Testament book, we find God showing Daniel visions of the last days of earth's history—think of it as the ultimate movie trailer. At one point God tells Daniel, " 'For 2,300 evenings and mornings. Then the sanctuary shall be restored to its rightful state [cleansed]' " (Daniel 8:14). Many have attempted during our church's history to determine which sanctuary God was talking about here. One gentleman named William Miller studied this Bible passage with a passion. He concluded that the 2,300 days started in 457 B.C. with the decree to rebuild the Israelite sanctuary, based on some other texts in Daniel such as chapter 9, verse 25.

So where does 2,300 days take us? Well, if you take them as literal twenty-four-hour days—nowhere. No significant historical happening signaled anything unusual taking place in the Israelite sanctuary in roughly 451 B.C., which is 2,300 literal days after 457 B.C. Not to mention that the rebuilt Jewish sanctuary at Jerusalem wasn't destroyed until A.D. 70. So you can't very well "restore" something that isn't in disrepair.

William Miller continued his study and stumbled upon a principle in the Bible (look at Numbers 14:34) that helps us understand time periods in prophecy. The principle is that each day mentioned in prophecy equals one literal year. So from 457 B.C. we skip all the way down to the year A.D. 1844.

As you can imagine, this was exciting news to William Miller, since he discovered it just a few years before 1844. Unfortunately for Mr. Miller, he made a little boo-boo. While he had the date pinpointed to 1844, he misinterpreted the sanctuary as referring to planet Earth. To him this meant that the cleansing of the sanctuary was equivalent to Jesus' second coming. And guess what happened in 1844?

Look around you—are you still on planet Earth? It's a shame, isn't it? And Will Miller was even more disappointed when Jesus didn't come. After restudying a bit and looking at some passages in Hebrews, some of Miller's followers, with the help of some scholars, determined that Christ entered His second phase of ministry in the *heavenly* sanctuary in 1844. This is His final phase, His judgment phase, before He returns to take His people home. It's a phase we call the investigative judgment.

"Investigative judgment" simply means this: Jesus is in His last phase of ministry in the heavenly sanctuary, and He is looking over the

What We Believe

heavenly record books to see who is and who isn't on His side. It makes sense. When Jesus comes back, the Bible says, "the dead in Christ will rise first. Then we who are alive . . . will be caught up together with them in the clouds to meet the Lord in the air, and so we will always be with the Lord" (1 Thessalonians 4:16, 17). And then "since indeed God considers it just to repay with affliction those who afflict you, . . . when the Lord Jesus is revealed from heaven with his mighty angels in flaming fire, [he will inflict] vengeance on those who do not know God and on those who do not obey the gospel of our Lord Jesus" (2 Thessalonians 1:6–8).

How could He inflict vengeance on the wicked unless He had made His judgments beforehand? No judge hands out sentences and then has the trial. The judgment is made first, and then the execution of judgment is carried out. Make sense? It's both exciting and creepy to think about, because on the one hand Jesus being in His final phase of ministry means He is coming back soon! On the other hand, if Jesus is in the middle of an investigative judgment, it means He is reviewing my case and making judgment about me.

I always dreaded the day in school when we discovered our grades. The teacher would stand at the desk and open that hefty grade book so the records of our performance—or lack of performance—could be seen.

A hush would fall over the class as one by one the names were called out and students made their way to the teacher. We all wanted to see who would sing the song of salvation (a good grade), give the sigh of suffering (not quite a good grade), or simply take the slow walk of shame back to their desk ("see you this summer"). Usually for me it was one of the last two responses.

Without fail, the pupils in academic peril would cry out to the teacher: "Extra credit! For the love of all that is good and decent, give us extra credit!"

If the teacher had a soul they would look into the teary eyes of the quivering-lipped students—feel their pain—and give them extra-credit work that would improve the lamenting learners' grades. Unfortunately, most times the teacher wasn't so kind, or the students did the extra-credit work at the same level of their regular work—it didn't get done at all.

Revelation 14:7 says, " 'the hour of his judgment has come.' " Your life is being graded right now. How comforting is that? The Bible gives us comforting words regarding judgment of those raised to life at the end of time. "Another book was opened, which is the book of life. The dead were judged according to what they had done as recorded in the books . . . and each person was judged according to what he had done" (Revelation 20:12b, 13, NIV). Judged—graded—according to what we've done.

Thinking about our heavenly grades gives me the heebie-jeebies. How many times have we been absent when God needed us? What was our attitude the last time we were asked to participate in church? Just how many failing marks do we have when it comes to worship and wanting to spend time with God instead of television? We need extra credit. We need so much extra credit that even if we had perfect church attendance, gave everything to the homeless, prayed ten hours a day, read the Bible five hours, walked stray dogs for another five, and then spent the rest of the day hugging and kissing the ugliest people we could find, we *still* wouldn't come close to even a passing grade.

Thankfully our Teacher Jesus knows how pitiful we are. When He was on earth He lived the perfect grade-A life, even though He was tempted, hurt, and betrayed by those who loved Him. "For we do not have a high priest who is unable to sympathize with our weaknesses, but we have one who has been tempted in every way, just as we are—yet was without sin" (Hebrews 4:15, NIV). The best part is that Jesus ascended to heaven to apply His grades to our permanent record in heaven. "How much more, then, will the blood of Christ, who . . . offered himself unblemished to God, cleanse our consciences from acts that lead to death" (Hebrews 9:14, NIV). Divine extra credit, you might say. I'm glad I have Jesus for a Teacher; because I never worry about my grades. I just need to follow His instructions in the Bible and ask for extra credit when I need it. I know He will never fail me.

25 | The Second Coming

He had never been so disappointed in his life. After years of studying the Bible, holding meetings, and convincing thousands of people that October 22, 1844, was the date Jesus would return to earth, William Miller could scarcely believe that he was staring into an empty sky.

Some people waited until midnight on October 22, but the only thing that happened was the breaking of hearts. A man named Henry Emmons, one of those waiting to see Jesus return, recounted his experience: "And dear Jesus did not come;—I waited all the forenoon of Wednesday, and was well in body as I ever was, but after 12 o'clock I began to feel faint, and before dark I needed some one to help me up to my chamber, as my natural strength was leaving me very fast, and I lay prostrate for 2 days without any pain—sick with disappointment."*

He was not the only one to be grief-stricken when Jesus did not return. Writing of the general experience of those who were waiting for Jesus to come back, Hiram Edson penned, "Our fondest hopes and expectations were blasted, and such a spirit of weeping came over us as

---

Day Star, Oct. 25, 1845.

The Second Coming

I never experienced before. It seemed that the loss of all earthly friends could have been no comparison. We wept and wept, till the day dawn."* Things were pretty bleak, to put it mildly, for those waiting for Jesus to return.

While most people stopped setting dates for Jesus' second coming at that point, some kept trying to set a date when Jesus would come back. They were disappointed every time. Thankfully, in spite of the disappointment, many regrouped and restudied and continued their wait for Jesus to come back. Some of them formed the Seventh-day Adventist Church, whose name (Adventist) indicates people who are waiting for the second advent (second coming) of Jesus. More than 150 years later, we are still waiting for Jesus to come back.

While it is true that Jesus has not yet appeared, we still cling to that wonderful promise in the Bible. " 'Let not your hearts be troubled. Believe in God; believe also in me. In my Father's house are many rooms. If it were not so, would I have told you that I go to prepare a place for you? And if I go and prepare a place for you, I will come again and will take you to myself, that where I am you may be also' " (John 14:1–3).

But people are beginning to get tired of hearing that Jesus is coming back. Some *Christians* are starting to get weary of waiting for Jesus to come back. Recently while online I came across a number of sites that are trying to convince people that Jesus is *not* coming back. One site even claimed to be able to prove it from the Bible.

I have also heard a discouraging response to preachers when they talk about the Second Coming. They will preach their message, saying Jesus is coming soon, and the people say, "Yeah, yeah. I heard that growing up, and so did my *grand*parents. Who knows when He's coming. . . ." Not an overwhelmingly positive response.

So what do we do? While we can see evidence from history and archaeology that biblical events such as the Flood really happened and biblical people such as Daniel, Paul, and Jesus existed, we have no historical data for the Second Coming—it hasn't happened yet. It's the one event in the Bible that has not yet come to pass.

---

*Hiram Edson, undated manuscript of his life and experience.

What We Believe

It reminds me of when I used to wait for my ride to pick me up from school. I'd finish a long, hard day of reading, writing, and arithmetic, and at three o'clock there was nothing more I wanted than to go home. At the end of the day I would have picked going home over five hundred bucks—that's how bad I wanted to get out of that wretched learning institution. I crammed all my books into my bag, put on my coat, and ran to the lobby, where the other hopefuls waited for their rides to come sweep them far, far away from their educational prison.

Some days, my ride would be waiting promptly outside. Leaving the school, I felt as though I had waited an eternity, and then I waved to the other poor saps still waiting as my car drove off toward home and an after-school snack. However, I wasn't always this lucky.

I can remember many times sitting there waiting from thirty minutes to an hour for my ride to come. It was the worst. After around twenty minutes, teachers began offering all sorts of "fun" things to do like clap out erasers, vacuum the floors, and other forms of manual labor they didn't want to do but got paid for.

It was the closest thing to eternity I have ever experienced. I would stare out the glass doors, looking down the vacant road, hoping for a glimpse of an automobile, a motorcycle, or even bicycle for crying out loud. I just wanted to go home. Finally, after a miserable hour, my ride would show up and I would refuse to answer the question—along with my fellow carpoolers—"So, how was your day, kids?"

People have been waiting for two *thousand* years for Jesus to come back. That's a long time for humans. No wonder they are getting tired of waiting. But that doesn't mean Jesus has left us high and dry with one little promise and no evidence or indication that He intends on fulfilling it. On the contrary, we have evidence that He is in the process of delivering on His promise.

First of all, in regard to the people losing heart and claiming there will be no Second Coming, the Bible has that covered: "Scoffers will come in the last days with scoffing, following their own sinful desires. They will say, 'Where is the promise of his coming? For ever since the fathers fell asleep, all things are continuing as they were from the

The Second Coming

beginning of creation.' . . . But do not overlook this one fact, beloved, that with the Lord one day is as a thousand years, and a thousand years as one day. The Lord is not slow to fulfill his promise as some count slowness, but is patient toward you, not wishing that any should perish" (2 Peter 3:3, 4, 8, 9). Surprisingly, the fact that people *are* getting tired of waiting is a sign that Christ is coming soon, even though God says He is waiting so that more people have the chance to be saved. And there's more.

When Jesus' disciples asked Him about the end of time, He told them that, while they couldn't know the exact date, they could recognize the signs. Just like the leaves changing color tells us winter is coming, changes will happen in the world that give us a clue as to the nearness of the Second Coming.

Jesus again: " 'And you will hear of wars and rumors of wars. For nation will rise against nation, and there will be famines and earthquakes in various places. . . . And because lawlessness will be increased, the love of many will grow cold. But the one who endures to the end will be saved' " (Matthew 24:6, 7, 12, 13). So are these sorts of things happening? I'm sure you don't need to see them, but just check out a few statistics on what is happening in the world.

First there is the whole idea of war. I just checked today's headlines, and the first thing I saw was an article titled, "Iran president says Israel's days are numbered." In this cheery article the president of Iran calls for wiping out the entire Jewish nation. And this is just one of many such articles. I did an online search with the word *war* as a keyword, and it pulled up more than thirty-three hundred results. That's just in one day! I bet that no matter when you read this, you could go online and pull up just as many wars and rumors of wars. War is a sign of Christ's coming, and we can see it everywhere.

The second sign mentioned in Matthew 24 has to do with famine and earthquakes—two items that we are in no shortage of. It is estimated that in the twentieth century alone, seventy million people died as a result of famine. As we make our way through the twenty-first century, many areas of the world are still suffering from famines. One of the most frightening statistics in the world today is that six million

What We Believe

children under the age of five die every year as a result of hunger. And we haven't even gotten to earthquakes yet.

According to studies of the year 2000, there were 22,256 earthquakes that year, resulting in 231 deaths. Just four years later there were 31,194 earthquakes and approximately 284,010 deaths. That is an incredible leap. One of the reasons was that the earth witnessed the second worst earthquake in recorded history. With the force of twenty-three thousand atomic bombs, it caused the death of well over two hundred thousand people and caused seven and a half billion dollars' worth of damage. The earth appears to be getting ready for the second coming of Christ.

Finally the text talks about lawlessness and people's love growing cold. I'll let you be the judge of this one—where do you see people's love growing cold? In what ways do you think lawlessness has increased? I'll even challenge you to look inside your church. Do you see Christians becoming more or less friendly and loving? Do you think Christians are becoming less or more concerned about the law—both God's and man's?

> *All the signs mentioned in Matthew 24 have been around since the first sin entered the world. What do you think is the difference between the signs now and the ones back then?*

Finally, another encouragement to us as we wait for Jesus is to look at the history of God's people in the Bible. One account that reminds me of waiting for the Second Coming is the story of Noah. He was a guy who lived in a world even more filled with sin than ours. The Bible says that even the purpose of the thoughts of people was evil. So God decided to undo His creation by sending a worldwide flood to destroy it and all the people too. Except Noah.

Noah found grace in God's eyes, and as a result God decided to rescue him by having him build a huge boat that would help him and his family survive the Flood. In a sense it was like waiting for the Second Coming—Noah was waiting for God to send the rain to destroy wickedness and carry him and his family to safety.

The Second Coming

It took 120 years of building—and fruitless preaching to the wicked people—before God finally said it was time to get into the boat. One hundred twenty years of preparation—it almost makes you wonder if Noah began to question whether or not God was serious about what He had said. Day after day, year after year, decade after decade, Noah waited, looking up at the sky—and now the time had finally come.

"Then the LORD said to Noah, 'Go into the ark, you and all your household, for I have seen that you are righteous before me in this generation. . . . For in seven days I will send rain on the earth forty days and forty nights, and every living thing that I have made I will blot out from the face of the ground.' And Noah did all that the LORD had commanded him. . . . And after seven days the waters of the flood came upon the earth" (Genesis 7:1, 4, 5, 10).

Notice two things here. First, even after Noah and his family got into the ark, there was more waiting! Can you imagine just sitting in the ark for a week with not so much as a crack of thunder or a drop of rain hitting the ark? What do you think went through Noah's mind? Was this some sort of cruel joke? This is a lesson in being patient and trusting in God right up to the very end—something God challenges us to do. "You too, be patient and stand firm, because the Lord's coming is near" (James 5:8, NIV).

The second lesson from the past is that God does what He promises. The Flood came, and Noah and his family floated to a new life away from the wickedness they had been living in. The Bible tells us that God's Word doesn't return empty (check Isaiah 55:10). We can read in the Bible and reflect on our own experiences with God—how He has been faithful to us—and we can know that He indeed will come back again to take us home.

Like the Flood, Jesus' coming will be literal, visible, and worldwide. "For the Lord himself will descend from heaven with a cry of command, with the voice of an archangel, and with the sound of the trumpet of God. And the dead in Christ will rise first. Then we who are alive, who are left, will be caught up together with them in the clouds to meet the Lord in the air, and so we will always be with the Lord"

(1 Thessalonians 4:16, 17). When Jesus invades the world for the second time, it will be the loudest, brightest, and grandest thing anyone has ever seen. And everyone will see it—it's not going to be a secret.

"Look, he is coming with the clouds, and every eye will see him, even those who pierced him; and all the peoples of the earth will mourn because of him. So shall it be! Amen" (Revelation 1:7, NIV).

So what can we do to pass the time while we wait and hope for Jesus' return? Well, we can do more than mope about it or just stare at the sky wondering when our heavenly "ride" is coming to pick us up to take us home. One of the signs that will indicate the nearness of Jesus' return is that the gospel will be preached to the entire world (look at Matthew 24:14).

We can spend the time we have left on earth sharing the message that Jesus' coming is sooner than it has ever been. We can keep ourselves busy telling others of God's love and His plans for those who will follow Him. And while we can't set a specific date for the blessed hope we have in Jesus, we can watch as the signs of His coming grow more and more intense; we can reflect on how faithful He has been in the past, and we can know that when it comes to Jesus keeping His promises, we will never be disappointed.

26 | Death and Resurrection

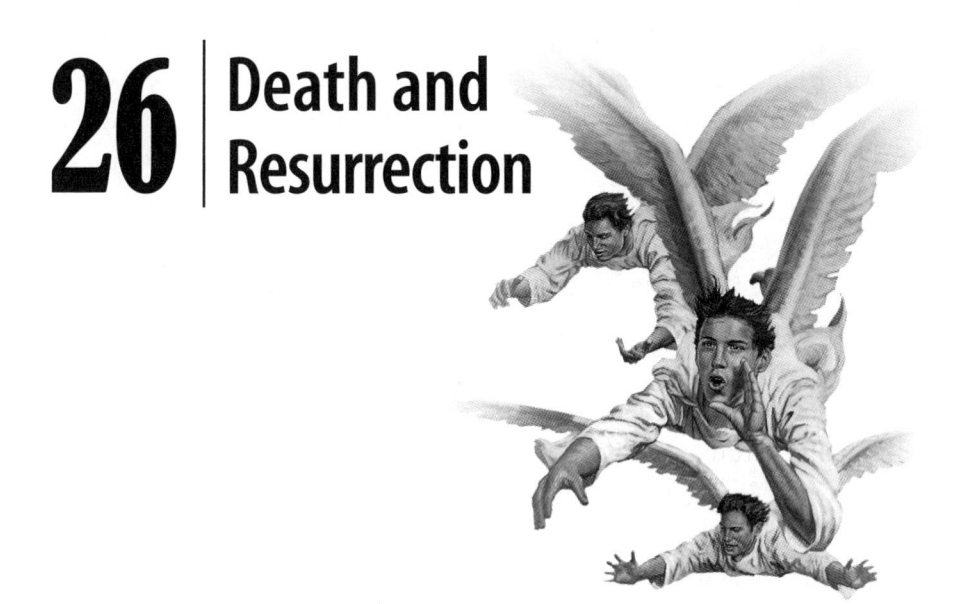

A couple of years ago I went to the doctor to have my first surgery. I had broken my jaw in a football game (I think we won, so it's OK), and it required me to see a specialist called a maxillofacial surgeon. I was told the day before that he would just assess the damage and then we would set a date for the operation to fix my jaw. That's what I was told.

What actually happened was that I went into the surgeon's office and sat in a chair like they have at the dentist's office, and the surgeon took a look at my injury. So far, so good, right? Well, then he said, "OK, just lie back, and we should have you done in a couple of hours."

"What?" I exclaimed as best I could with a busted jaw.

"Yeah, we should have you done in a short while—are you allergic to anesthesia?"

Anesthesia. I had heard about it from other people—they seemed to have a good experience generally. It put them into a deep sleep and they felt or knew nothing, and then they woke up and went home. But I was *not* prepared that day. The idea of having a needle in my arm pumping a substance that would put me "under" was just a little unnerving,

What We Believe

mainly because I had signed a form which said they weren't responsible if I died from an adverse reaction to the substance. *Died* is seldom a comforting word, especially when it relates to you.

As a nurse leaned my chair back and then put the needle into my arm, I couldn't help feeling panic at what it would feel like to slip into the oncoming darkness.

There are many ideas in the world about what happens when a person dies. Some people say that after death you go straight to heaven or hell, while others say that you are reincarnated (or reborn) as an animal or another person; still others say that absolutely nothing happens after you die—that's it, the end, no more. But the Bible gives us an entirely different picture of death.

"For the living know that they will die, but the dead know nothing" (Ecclesiastes 9:5, NIV). The Bible clearly says that after you die, you're not thinking about anything. No dreams, no meditations, no thoughts. Death means that your mind ceases to function. Cheery, huh?

I don't remember when the anesthetic overtook me as I lay in that surgery chair. It just . . . happened. No warning, no pain, and strangely enough, no dreams. It was really weird, and it's hard to describe unless you've experienced it. It's like you disappear; you cease to exist; you are just . . . nothing.

Thankfully it didn't stay that way. I woke up. And when Jesus talked to others about death He let people know that although their loved ones were in a state where they knew nothing, they were not going to stay that way.

One of Jesus' friends died. His name was Lazarus. Naturally Lazarus's friends were upset, and they approached Jesus about it. That's when He said something interesting. "He said to them, 'Our friend Lazarus has fallen asleep, but I go to awaken him'" (John 11:11). Uh, asleep? So he's not dead? Those around Jesus found His statement to be a little hard to understand, as you can imagine.

"The disciples said to him, 'Lord, if he has fallen asleep, he will recover'" (verse 12). "No big deal, Jesus. If Lazarus is asleep, let's just let him rest. Just get the man some soup and fluff his pillow and he should be good, right?"

Death and Resurrection

"Now Jesus had spoken of his death, but they thought that he meant taking rest in sleep" (verse 13). Well, apparently the man *is* dead, and for some reason Jesus refers to it as being asleep. He says even stranger things when He encounters Lazarus's sister Martha.

"So when Martha heard that Jesus was coming, she went and met him, but Mary remained seated in the house. Martha said to Jesus, 'Lord, if you had been here, my brother would not have died.' . . . Jesus said to her, 'Your brother will rise again . . . and everyone who lives and believes in me shall never die. Do you believe this?' " (verses 20, 21, 23, 26). Huh? Rise again? Maybe Jesus was just upset. I mean, Lazarus was Jesus' friend as well, after all. But this isn't the only time when Jesus says something strange during a time of mourning for a departed loved one.

Jesus was once approached by someone right in the middle of a sermon. The man's name was Jairus, and he was heartbroken because his daughter was very sick. He begged Jesus to come and heal her. Jesus agreed and headed out with the man, but as they drew near to the house where the sick little girl was, a servant ran out to tell Jairus and Jesus, " 'Your daughter is dead. Why trouble the Teacher any further?' " (Mark 5:35).

It seems like a perfectly logical thing to say. If the girl is dead, then it's all over. She's gone and "knows nothing," as the Bible says. Everyone should just begin funeral preparations, right? But that's not the end of this story.

"But overhearing what they said, Jesus said to the ruler of the synagogue, 'Do not fear, only believe.' . . . They came to the house of the ruler of the synagogue, and Jesus saw a commotion, people weeping and wailing loudly. And when he had entered, he said to them, 'Why are you making a commotion and weeping? The child is not dead but sleeping' " (verses 36, 38, 39). Now if you were at a funeral for someone you loved and someone stood up and said, "They're just sleeping," what would your reaction be? That's how these people reacted as well. "And they laughed at him" (verse 40). It really is an absurd thing to say, wouldn't you agree? Asleep? Just an extended nap? Is that really all it is? How would you have reacted? The people couldn't understand. They had witnessed the fever, the coughing, the girl's little body wracked with suffering as, bit by bit, her life was squeezed out by the sickness. There was nothing left. A nap? Yeah, right.

Jesus wasn't impressed with the laughter. He is too loving to make jokes at such a painful time in the lives of His children. He is the same One who fashioned human existence, healed the sick, and embraced little children when others tried to send them away. We can only assume that He was serious in what He said.

Jesus politely removed everyone from the room where the little girl lay "sleeping," and then He proved that His definition of death as a sleep was more accurate than the hopeless picture in the mind of those around Him. "Taking her by the hand he said to her, 'Talitha cumi,' which means, 'Little girl, I say to you, arise' " (verse 41).

Jesus said almost exactly the same thing to His friend Lazarus as He stood in front of the tomb he had been put in four days earlier. "When he had said these things, he cried out with a loud voice, 'Lazarus, come out' " (John 11:43).

So what was the result? Were they reincarnated already? Did they just stay dead? Were they in heaven or hell? In both situations we have the same result:

"And immediately the girl got up and began walking (for she was twelve years of age), and they were immediately overcome with amazement" (Mark 5:42).

"The man [Lazarus] who had died came out, his hands and feet bound with linen strips, and his face wrapped with a cloth. Jesus said to them, 'Unbind him, and let him go' " (John 11:44).

When I woke up after the surgery on my jaw, I tried really hard to remember when exactly I fell asleep. I tried to remember any feelings or thoughts I had, but there was nothing there. It was like someone hit a Pause button on my life and then pressed Play again. All I knew now was that I was awake and could go home (actually I had to get wheeled out to the car, because anesthesia makes you a little loopy). It was a weird and amazing experience. I ceased to be, and then—*Poof!*—I was back. Only those who have had surgery know what I'm talking about.

You can imagine the thoughts of Lazarus and the little girl—trying to figure out what had just happened to them, because as far as they knew they had just closed their eyes for a split second. When they awoke they both saw Jesus and realized that they had been brought back from the sleep of death.

No doubt they would have been upset had they been in heaven and been forced to come back to earth. And if they had been sinful enough to go straight to hell there would have been no point in bringing them back. All this tells me that Jesus knew what He was saying when He likened death to a sleep.

This is a hard thing for some people to grasp, because so many people believe their loved one goes straight to heaven after they die. No doubt this is a comforting thought to them—after all, being with God in heaven is where we all want to be. But besides seeing Jesus refer to death as being asleep and how the Bible refers to the dead as not knowing anything (I would prefer to know I was in heaven if I were there), the idea of going straight to heaven or hell just isn't as nice a thought as people think. Let me explain.

Have you ever been to a bad talent show? I mean, a talent show full of people who thought they had talent but they didn't? I have been to several and even hosted one. Let me tell you, it is one of the most painful things in the world to watch, especially if people you know and like are involved. I have seen everything from lip syncing out of synch to dancing that was more seizure than dance to puppet shows without puppets and jokes that were not funny. When your loved one is engaged in their act, it is so horrible you just want to crawl under the stage and hide until it's all over—or call a time-out and explain to your friend that what they are doing is causing you a great amount of mental, physical, and spiritual pain and they need to stop.

Now imagine being in heaven and looking down on your loved ones as they stumble through life, get hurt, get embarrassed, and get very sick. Heaven wouldn't be much fun if the only TV was "The World of Sin Channel: Where Everyone Gets Hurt and Hurts Each Other." I'd rather be dead.

And thinking back to my surgery, while the surgeon was slicing and stitching and putting the titanium plate in my jaw, I was completely oblivious. Had I been awake, it would have been a horrifically painful experience, and even if I couldn't feel it, the sights and sounds of what they were doing no doubt would be just as awful. I'm glad I was asleep.

Jesus promises that death is not permanent for those who love Him. It is an unconscious sleep—a soul sleep if you like—where your life's energy goes back to God and you remain at rest until He comes again to raise you from the dead.

" 'Whoever feeds on my flesh and drinks my blood [reference to the Lord's Supper] has eternal life, and I will raise him up on the last day' " (John 6:54).

A year after my surgery I had to go back to the same surgeon to have my wisdom teeth removed. This is a fun procedure where they cut out four teeth in the back of your mouth and then cram cotton balls back there to stop all the bleeding. Most people have to get it done, so there is something for you to get excited about if you haven't had them out yet. Anyway, I was going to have to get put under again. This time, however, I wasn't nervous. I understood what it meant to be put under. And as the needle went into my arm again, I smiled, lay back, and simply closed my eyes in waiting. The next thing I knew, I was being raised into an upright position. It went quickly, and I didn't feel a thing. I wish I could have anesthesia during other parts of my life, such as midterms and finals, waiting in lines, and even some sermons I've heard.

The point is, I'm not scared to get put under anymore. And when we understand death for what it is—anesthesia for the soul—it isn't so scary anymore. We can face the reality of death with confidence because we know with Jesus it is only a sleep. When we die we can trust Him to wake us up in time to see His magnificent return. He won't let us oversleep.

"For the Lord himself will descend from heaven with a cry of command, with the voice of an archangel, and with the sound of the trumpet of God. And the dead in Christ will rise first" (1 Thessalonians 4:16).

27 | The Millennium and the End of Sin

There was no escaping it. The pain. The relentless, merciless, and pitiless pain gnawing into my gums like a hungry dog gnaws a bone. What started as a mildly sensitive tooth in the afternoon now snarled into a full-blown toothache at 3:00 A.M. And it was angry.

To make matters worse, we had no more painkillers (which I had been happily popping like candies since supper). It was no use. Despite having school in just a short time, and being in a stupor of sleep deprivation and agony, I had to get up and find medicine.

Since the little town in which we lived had only two grocery stores and neither was open twenty-four hours, I would have to find a gas station. There were three in town, and the third one I went to was open. By this time, my mouth felt as though it was going to explode. I bought the medicine swiftly, drove home, and promptly took as many pills as the label on the bottle would allow. It helped, but not completely. I had a fitful sleep trying to dream away the dull throb that persisted until four hours later, when the pain flared up again.

I made an appointment with the dentist first thing in the morning. The receptionist said he could see me first thing—on Tuesday! Two whole days away! I was going to die. I knew it. I knew that the bottom half of my face would eventually fall off, and whatever was causing the grief would spread to the rest of my body, and it would be curtains for me.

I didn't sleep much during that time. For crying out loud, how could a tiny tooth cause such tremendous suffering? I had to leave class because I couldn't focus, and I was dizzy from the pills I had to keep taking to make the pain bearable.

When I finally got into the dentist, he told me I was the lucky winner of a root canal. This is a sweet little surgery where they dope you up, drill down into the root of your tooth, clean out the diseased pulp, and refill it. It feels as good as it sounds. But I was desperate—anything to stop the pain!

I spent an hour and a half in the dentist's chair staring at the ceiling while I was poked and prodded by shiny spiked objects. When it was all over, my decaying tooth root was cleansed and fixed. I was set free from my pain and agony.

However, as awful as the pain caused by a bad tooth is—and it is *bad*—it is only an insignificant sample of the pain happening in the world because of sin and evil. Heartaches are far worse than toothaches, and this planet is chock full of them.

Just today I read that a suicide attack killed four people in Somalia. Apparently a few people loaded up a car with explosives and drove it into some other cars. I wonder if there were any parents or children lost in that attack, or what kind of heartache the killers must have been feeling to do such a thing. Another news story said that a man in London was charged with killing a baby girl. No doubt the heartache the family feels is devastating. These examples of killing and murder, as horrible as they are, amount to insignificant samples of all the pain of hatred and death in the world. Millions die each year, and not just because of war or murder, but just because they get old. None of us can live forever on this planet. Even if we manage a long life here, we have other pain to consider.

Statistics tell us that every forty seconds a child is kidnapped in America, taken from their home and family against their will. This amounts to somewhere around 788,000 kids every year. Nearly a million homes ripped apart. This is an increase of 444 percent since 1892. And if murder and kidnapping weren't enough to make the world a painful place, we have diseases to worry about.

I'm not sure how many forms of disease there are, but I bet the number is high enough to make you sick. Just to give you some of the horrible highlights, look at these statistics:

- In 2006 more than five hundred thousand people died of cancer. That's about fourteen hundred people per day.
- Roughly forty million people in the world have AIDS, an incurable disease that attacks the immune system. Three million of them are children.

Then you can't forget all the people who are addicted to alcohol and other drugs, and to other destructive lifestyles that are about as easy to stop as stopping a fall in midair. And if all the health issues we face from sicknesses weren't enough, we have to factor in poverty.

Nearly three billion people live on less than two dollars per day. According to UNICEF, thirty thousand children die each day due to poverty. And they "die quietly in some of the poorest villages on earth, far removed from the scrutiny and the conscience of the world. Being meek and weak in life makes these dying multitudes even more invisible in death."

I think you are getting the point. I haven't even mentioned natural disasters, divorce, hunger, or all the times that we just aren't nice to each other. We live on a planet full of pain. Statistics show that it isn't getting any better. And while there are still beautiful parts to our world and also beautiful people, it is getting harder to deny that our world is decaying like a rotten tooth. Someone needs to do something. Something needs to happen. And that Someone to do something is Jesus.

When Jesus comes again, the Bible tells us, an angel will bind the devil to this earth. The planet will be made desolate. Those who died while following Jesus on earth "came to life and reigned with Christ a thousand years . . . and holy are those who have part in the first

What We Believe

resurrection . . . but they will be priests of God and of Christ and will reign with him for a thousand years" (Revelation 20:4, 6, NIV).

Jesus will come back and take us to reign with Him in heaven for one thousand years. A thousand years? In heaven? I can't wait. The longest break from suffering I ever got was back when I still had summer vacation from school. It was a time to set aside studies and just spend three months basking in the beautiful summer sun, free from my academic burdens. You may be one of the lucky ones who still have summer vacations. Listen to me closely—put off work as long as you can. Enjoy your summers! Live it up, relax, and sleep in till noon, because you will miss it like nothing else when it's gone. If I had a summer vacation now, it would be so foreign to me I'm not sure what I'd do. I'd probably cry.

No doubt there will be tears of joy in the eyes of God's followers when they go to heaven. But then what happens after the thousand years end? And what exactly will be going on down on our old friend planet Earth? Revelation gives us those answers as well.

"He seized the dragon, that ancient serpent, who is the devil, or Satan, and bound him for a thousand years. He threw him into the Abyss, and locked and sealed it over him, to keep him from deceiving the nations anymore until the thousand years were ended" (Revelation 20:2, 3, NIV). The devil is left alone to think about all the trouble he's caused on planet Earth (here referred to as the Abyss), because when Christ comes back, His glory is so powerful that the wicked are destroyed and the earth is left a desolate place. For a thousand years the devil wallows in a wasteland, while we are in heaven asking God questions and living in perfection with Jesus.

However, we don't stay in heaven forever. If you'll look at the last part of Revelation 20:3 you will see that the devil is kept from his deceptions "until the thousand years were ended." After a thousand years he makes a mad dash to reclaim his pain-racked way of life.

"When the thousand years are over, Satan will be released from his prison and will go out to deceive the nations in the four corners of the earth . . . to gather them for battle. In number they are like the sand on the seashore. They marched across the breadth of the earth and surrounded the camp of God's people, the city he loves" (Revelation 20:7–9, NIV). The devil is on the war path, and he comes after God's people as they return to the earth from heaven.

Now I've been depressed coming home from vacations before, but this scene has got to be the biggest letdown. I mean, it's one thing to come home and realize you have work to return to, a million messages on your answering machine, bills to be paid, school to get back to, or even just a house that you left in a mess as you dashed off to your vacation. But to come back from heaven, a perfect place, to countless legions of the wickedest evils that ever existed, all resurrected and led by Satan himself, is just a wee bit disappointing—and frightening.

But God doesn't take us to heaven for a thousand years to tease us and then bring us back to a broken world. He brings us back to witness as He makes things right once and for all, so we can live with Him in a new place where pain and sin could never make our hearts ache again. He's been promising it for a long time.

" 'Surely the day is coming; it will burn like a furnace. All the arrogant and every evildoer will be stubble,' . . . says the LORD Almighty. 'Not a *root* or a branch will be left to them' " (Malachi 4:1, NIV; emphasis added). I emphasize the word *root* because it reminds me of my tooth. God isn't just going to work on the surface to fix our problem of pain and sin. He is going to remove every decaying, rotten, sinful element that the world can muster. He'll burn it to nothing with holy fire: "Fire came down from heaven and devoured them. And the devil, who deceived them, was thrown into the lake of burning sulfur, where the beast and the false prophet had been thrown" (Revelation 20:9, 10, NIV). In describing this scene where the devil and all his evil minions are destroyed, Ellen White wrote, "Satan's work of ruin is forever ended. . . . Now God's creatures are forever delivered from his presence and temptations."*

God performs a divine root canal by fire. And while it will certainly be a sad moment to witness those who, if they had only trusted Jesus, could have avoided the flames, Jesus introduces to us another scene in Revelation that promises hope and comfort for the future:

---

*The Great Controversy, p. 673.

What We Believe

> Then I saw a new heaven and a new earth, for the first heaven and the first earth had passed away. . . . I saw the Holy City, the new Jerusalem, coming down out of heaven from God. . . . And I heard a loud voice from the throne saying, "Now the dwelling of God is with men, and he will live with them. They will be his people, and God himself will be with them and be their God. He will wipe every tear from their eyes. There will be no more death or mourning or crying or pain, for the old order of things has passed away" (Revelation 21:1–4, NIV).

The New Jerusalem—a city described as being encrusted with gems and whose streets are made from gold so fine that it is transparent—descends right out of heaven and plants itself onto the "new earth" that God has restored. It will strike awe into everyone who sees it, as it is the place God Himself designed just for us since the beginning of time.

The first time I saw Disney World, I was blown away. It was huge! It was full of color, music, dancing, delicious food, thrills, and happy people (except for the occasional child who would have a panic attack when he or she saw Mickey Mouse in person). No wonder they called it the "Happiest Place on Earth." I marveled at Cinderella's towering castle and howled with joy as I rode a ten-foot wave in Typhoon Lagoon. Considering I was in my "cool" stage of life, when I had long hair, wore all black, and frowned all the time because cool people weren't supposed to smile like a goofus, I found this place really amazing in its power to pump people full of happiness. This Magic Kingdom demanded happiness and good times—so much so that if anyone tells me they had a miserable time at Disney World, I offer to make a psychiatric appointment for them.

God's kingdom is even more impressive. Not to mention that the tickets are free and you never have to leave. Ever. We will spend eternity in a kingdom free from pain and sickness and full of love and the presence of God. God extends the invitation to you if you are just willing to accept it and let Him plan an eternal vacation free from sin forever.

28 | The New Earth

One of my favorite things to do when I am bored is look at pictures of beautiful homes and imagine what it would be like to own one. I have a bunch of favorite Web sites and free real estate papers that I enjoy looking at. You would not believe some of the houses out there.

One house I saw in Italy was known as the Costello Scotti—a *huge* castle with gardens, towers, battlements, and fireplaces so big that you could walk into them without having to duck. Of course it costs so much that they didn't even list the price—they ask you to call if you are serious. So perhaps we should consider something more affordable.

For a measly $110 million you can buy a ranch called Rancho El Cojo, located on the coast near beautiful Santa Barbara, California. It has nine miles of coastline, beautiful rolling green hills, mountains, and places to ride a whole fleet of horses if you wanted. Every friend you ever had plus everyone in your family could live there comfortably. But maybe ranches aren't your style—maybe you want something more isolated.

For the pittance of $75 million you can own your own tropical island in Fiji. You heard me—your own island. Totally secluded, private, and complete with your own white sandy beaches. The waters surrounding it are crystal clear blue. There are forests, flowers, and more fun than is probably healthy. What would you do with your own island?

You could live in a lot of cool places in this world. Cabins with enough land to start your own country, castles that would make King Arthur jealous, and mansions that have indoor pools, tennis courts, personal theaters, and more bathrooms than a person could ever dream of using (even after eating Taco Bell late at night). But there is another place we could live that outshines all of these options. No home on earth can compare to the one that God Himself is going to make. That's because it is quite literally out of this world. It is a new earth.

"Then I saw a new heaven and a new earth, for the first heaven and the first earth had passed away, and the sea was no more. And I saw the holy city, new Jerusalem, coming down out of heaven from God, prepared as a bride adorned for her husband" (Revelation 21:1, 2). Just like a person turning in their old car for a new one or an old house being torn down to build a new one in its place, God will literally replace this planet via the cleansing power of fire, and re-create it as a brand-new home world for His followers. But that's not all.

As I write this book, my wife and I are currently renting a duplex while we finish our master's degrees. It is a nice place that has everything we need—including a terrific landlord, or in our case a landlady. Her name is Virginia. Whenever something goes wrong with our house, such as a leaky faucet, broken toilet, or missing roof, we just give her a call and she sends help to come our way and fix it up for free. We really appreciate her a lot. But I must say she's limited—any landlord is limited.

See, even if I owned a castle, an island, or a ranch the size of China, I could still get hurt and have personal problems. I could fall down my stairs, get into a fight with my wife, or drown in my own personal pool. Even if I have a brand-new mansion, I still have the potential to commit sin and do something stupid. I could lie, drink gasoline, or light myself on fire. Can a landlord prevent that from happening? What about other people doing nasty things to me? My wife could punch me in the face, I could get robbed, or someone could drive their car into my living

The New Earth

room. No matter how good my house is, or how good my landlord is, they have no power to remove the sin in this world that could cause any number of problems. However, God has promised that the home He will make in the *new* earth will have the perfect landlord—the Land LORD.

> And I heard a loud voice from the throne saying, "Behold, the dwelling place of God is with man. He will dwell with them, and they will be his people, and God himself will be with them as their God. He will wipe away every tear from their eyes, and death shall be no more, neither shall there be mourning nor crying nor pain anymore, for the former things have passed away."
>
> And he who was seated on the throne said, "Behold, I am making all things new." Also he said, "Write this down, for these words are trustworthy and true" (Revelation 21:3–5).

God has promised to move right in with His people. We will live with the Creator of the universe. And He is such a good landlord that not only does He guarantee that everything will be made new but that all sin, pain, and suffering will be fixed. He has repaired things so well that they will never break again.

Our home will be perfect. There will be no more hate, only love. There will be no more unbelief, just worship and hope. And there will be no more sin, only salvation and safety. I can't wait until it's time to move into our new home—our new world. It will be a whole planet full of promise and possibility and no pain. That's a home more fun to look at and think about than any human habitat on earth.

More books to help children and adults understand the beliefs of the Seventh-day Adventist Church

What We Believe for Kids
Jerry D. Thomas

Jerry D. Thomas has turned his considerable talents to explaining what Seventh-day Adventists believe. Each of the twenty-eight fundamental beliefs is explained in a kid-friendly manner through a story from his own experience, an apt analogy, or retelling of a Bible story. Now when someone asks your children what church they go to, and they answer the Seventh-day Adventist Church, they will also be able to answer the next question: What do Adventists believe? (Ages 6–9)
Paperback, 80 pages.   0-8163-2167-1   US$11.99

Seventh-day Adventists Believe . . .
An exposition of the fundamental beliefs of the Seventh-day Adventist Church

Jesus, the central focus of Scripture and history, is also the central focus of Adventist doctrine and experience. In this dynamic book, the basic beliefs shared by Seventh-day Adventists are at your fingertips, ready to be explored, appraised, studied, and substantiated.

Seventh-day Adventists Believe . . . stands as an authentic resource on Adventist doctrine because it is written by Adventists themselves—more than 230 men and women were involved in the production of this book. Many of them contributed insights gained from years of study, prayer, and their personal walk with Jesus. (For adults)
Paperback, 468 pages.   1-57847-041-2   US$12.95

Beginning of the End
An adaptation of *Patriarchs and Prophets*

This is the first volume in a five-book series approved by the White Estate that will bring the clear messages of the Conflict of the Ages set to a new generation of readers. Biblical texts unless otherwise noted are taken from the New King James Version. Share the great truths of the original volumes in a more accessible format for twenty-first-century readers.
Paperback.   0-8163-2211-2   US$7.99

Order from your ABC by calling **1-800-765-6955**, or get online and shop our virtual store at **http//:www.AdventistBookCenter.com**.
• Read a chapter from your favorite book
• Order online
• Sign up for e-mail notices on new products

Prices subject to change without notice.